The God of Loneliness

Books by Philip Schultz

LIKE WINGS

DEEP WITHIN THE RAVINE

MY GUARDIAN ANGEL STEIN

THE HOLY WORM OF PRAISE

LIVING IN THE PAST

FAILURE

THE GOD OF LONELINESS

PHILIP SCHULTZ

The God of Loneliness

SELECTED AND NEW POEMS

Houghton Mifflin Harcourt

2010   BOSTON   NEW YORK

For information about permission to reproduce
selections from this book, write to Permissions,
Houghton Mifflin Harcourt Publishing Company,
215 Park Avenue South, New York, New York 10003.

www.hmhbooks.com

Library of Congress Cataloging-in-Publication Data
Schultz, Philip.
  The God of loneliness : selected and new poems / Philip Schultz.
    p. cm.
  Includes index.
  ISBN 978-0-547-24965-0
  I. Title.
  PS3569.C5533G63 2010
  811'.54—dc22   2009041895

Book design by Melissa Lotfy

Printed in the United States of America

DOC 10 9 8 7 6 5 4 3 2 1

To my wife, Monica,
and my sons, Eli and Augie

Being unable to cure death, wretchedness, and ignorance, men have decided, in order to be happy, not to think about such things.

—PASCAL

Contents

From *The Holy Worm of Praise*, 2002

From *Failure*, 2007

New Poems

Like Wings

1978

For the Wandering Jews

This room is reserved for wandering Jews.
Around me, in other rooms, suitcases whine
like animals shut up for the night.

My guardian angel, Stein, fears sleeping twice
in the same bed. Constancy brings Cossacks in the dark, he thinks.
You don't explain fear to fear. Despair has no ears, but teeth.

In the next room I hear a woman's laughter
& press my hand to the wall. Car lights burn
my flesh to a glass transparency.

My father was born in Novo-Nikolayevka, Ekaterinoslav Guberniya.
Like him, I wear my forehead high, have quick eyes, a belly laugh.
Miles unfold in the palm of my hand.

Across some thousand backyards his stone
roots him to the earth like a stake. Alone in bed,
I feel his blood wander through my veins.

As a boy I would spend whole nights at the fair
running up the fun house's spinning barrel toward its magical top,
where I believed I would be beyond harm, at last.

How I would break my body to be free of it,
night after night, all summer long, this boy climbing
the sky's turning side, against all odds,

as though to be one with time,
going always somewhere where no one had been before,
my arms banging at my sides like wings.

The Artist & His Mother: After Arshile Gorky

Such statuesque immobility; here we have it:
the world of form. Colors muted, a quality
of masks with fine high brows. Light & its absence.
Alchemy. The hands are unfinished. But what
could they hold? The transitory bliss
of enduring wonder? Mother, Mother & Son;
here we have it: consanguinity. The darkness
inside color. Space. In the beginning there was space.
It held nothing. What could it hold? Time?
The continuum? Mother & Son, forms suspended
in color. Silence. Her apron a cloud
of stillness swallowing her whole. Her eyes
roots of a darker dimension. Absence. Here we have it:
the world of absence. Light holds them in place.
The pulse of time is felt under the flesh,
the flesh of color. Continuum. You feel
such immensity. The anger of form. The woman
locked in the Mother; the man in the Son; the Son
in the Mother. Their hands do not touch. What
could they touch? Here we have it: the world
of gift. The gift too terrible to return. But
how could it be returned? In the beginning
there was anger. Mother & Son. The islands of time.
The passion to continue. Such statuesque immobility.
The hands, the hands cannot be finished.

The Stranger in Old Photos

You see him over my uncle Al's left shoulder
eating corn at a Sunday picnic & that's him
behind my parents on a boardwalk in Atlantic City

smiling out of focus like a rejected suitor
& he's the milkman slouched frozen crossing our old street
ten years before color & his is the face above mine in Times Square

blurring into the crowd like a movie extra's
& a darkness in his eyes as if he knew his face would outlast him
& he's tired of living on the periphery of our occasions.

These strangers at bus stops, sleepwalkers
caught forever turning a corner—I always wondered who they were
between photos when they weren't posing & if they mattered.

It's three this morning, a traffic light blinks yellow yellow
& in my window my face slips into the emptiness between glares.
We are strangers in our own photos. Our strangeness has no source.

Letter from Jake: August 1964

Never mind that uncle business my name is Jake.
In college they try every thing there is this girl
at Wegmans supermarket who is to busy to join
protests who is right takes more than me
to figure out. Cohen died last Monday. He owned
the deli on Joseph Ave. The democrat running
for supervisor is a Puerto Rican. Don't ask me why.

You are young and have to take things
as they come. Some day you will find your
real niche. I wrote poetry to but this July
I'm a stagehand 40 years. I've seen every movie
Paramount made believe me. Now theres a union
but I remember when you was happy just to work.
Meantime have a ball. Yrs truly now has kidney
trouble plus diabetic condition, heart murmur,
cataract in rt eye. Yr mother Lillian is well to.
Cohen was just 58. We went to school together. Loews
is closing in October. If you ask me the last
five rows was no good for cinemascope.

Yrs truly,

Jake

What I Don't Want

Die slouched & undecided in a girlie show
watching the lambs eat the wolves.
Sit talking Kafka this Kafka that
(that bugfaced sword-swallower!).
Play deaf & dumb in Chicago.
Chew the fat of the land while looking
up somebody's leg for the right word, ever again.
Cross the Golden Gate Bridge on a bus
listening to the guy ahead say: Doesn't it look
like a G-string all lit up, Fran!
Die in the house where I was born,
a happy man.

I want, Lord, to die with Neruda & Chaplin
naked & sinful
eating cheese so old it sings on my tongue.

The Elevator

This elevator lugged Teddy Roosevelt
when they both were new. Now I count stars
in the skylight as it jerks into the sudden light
down hallways & hug groceries like a thief his loot
when it stops in the dark between floors. Often
it howls climbing, sings falling. Someone
on the fifth floor loves chicken fat & Brahms;
the worst soprano in Cambridge lives on the third.
The man above me taps goodnight on his floor but
doesn't know me in the street. The girl down the hall
drops her head if I smile in the elevator; she knows
I watch her run to work each morning from my window.
After dinner I stand there with my hands folded behind
as I imagine Mr. Roosevelt stood, watching the lights
come on along the spine that is Massachusetts Avenue at night.

For the Moose

Tania must place her hands on my skull,
one above the other, to better hear the truth.
We are discussing the art of poetry. Eight
years old, she chews her lip & squints. Who's
my moose? she wants to know. Does she just
hand one over or what? Last night she dreamed
her bed was full of frogs, then her ship sank.
Do poems give nightmares? Funny, I say, but
I had the same dream. This breaks her up.
Well how about God; do you always have to put
Him in? No more than three-legged horses, I say.
They get equal time. Which brings the big one:
Will she be rich & famous before she's fifteen?
Will they hang her picture in the A&P?
Will she have to fall in love every day &
come down with some fatal disease? Her father
said poets led sad lives. I put my arms around
her & think: Stick to new math & somersaults
& if you must write, write historical novels
about gorgeous queens who give up whole kingdoms
for love. But say: Tania, your hair's on fire,
your eyes are poached eggs! So she punches me,
which means that's it for today. I watch her
go down the cinderblock with her hands high
on her head as if feeling a poem bake.
Darling, may the good moose be kind.

...cisco Remembered

In summer the polleny light bounces off the white buildings
& you can see their spines & nerves & where the joints knot.
You've never seen such polleny light. The whole city shining
& the women wearing dresses so thin you see their wing-tipped hips
& their tall silvery legs alone can knock your eye out.
But this isn't about women. It's about the city of blue waters
& fog so thick it wraps round your legs & leaves glistening trails
along the dark winding streets. Once I followed such a trail
& wound up beside this redheaded woman who looked up & smiled
& let me tell you you don't see smiles like that in Jersey City.
She was wearing a black raincoat with two hundred pockets
& I wanted to put my hands in each one. But forget about her.
I was talking about the fog which steps up & taps your shoulder
like a panhandler who wants bus fare to a joint called The Paradise
& where else could this happen? On Sundays Golden Gate Park
is filled with young girls strolling the transplanted palms
& imported rhododendron beds. You should see the sunset
in their eyes & the sway, the proud sway of their young shoulders.
Believe me, it takes a day or two to recover. Or the trolleys clanking
down the steep hills—why you see legs flashing like mirrors!
Please, Lord, please let me talk about San Francisco. How
that gorilla of a bridge twists in the ocean wind & the earth
turns under your feet & at any moment the whole works can crack
& slip back into the sea like a giant being kicked off his raft
& now, if it's all right, I would like to talk about women . . .

Onionskin: For the New Year

Already there is as much behind as ahead.
Knowing this we link arms, here, high
on the cusp of the city, in the vicinity
of this moment. Refugees, we strain
for a glimpse of the New World, ready
to astonish any absolute. Below,
the Charles spins its sinuous flow
of detail under bridges of pure reason
as we smile for the gap-toothed honey
who snaps us for posterity. Yes,
it has become impossible to be human;
we agree that we are what is good
about time & sing for all we're worth,
our whisky gargle the unraveling onionskin
of too many near collisions.

The Gift

For Ralph Dickey, 1945–1972

All that night the sere-faced moon drifted
through gray islands of sky as we tightroped
the reservoir's edge tossing stones & listening
for the tiny handclaps of water & later
we went down to the frozen river where he hopped one-legged
over cracking water with such laughter I think
he believed we would live forever in our bodies.

He never saw his black father
& his blond mother left him when his hair curled to wool
& he was left again when his almond-colored flesh turned cinnamon
& again until a black mother said with hands like his
he must play piano & nights he jammed with old black men
in tenement basements tapping his foot & keeping time with spoons
& it was so good, this music, it lifted him right out of his body.

There were nights he would call late & play something new
& hang up without hello or good-bye & the air rang electric
& this morning I saw his face in every face in a crowd
& wished I could have told him the mystery of our lives unfolding,
the eyes of these women, their bodies coats of such blossoming color.

His body was found in the back seat of an old VW
parked on a cliff by the Pacific & a plastic bag
was wrapped round his head like the stocking he wore to flatten his hair
& his stomach was shredded with snail poison & his hands,
his hands large as Rachmaninoff's, were frozen to his throat
as if to feel the last singing breath.

One night I drove to those cliffs
where, below, the surf burns blue in the moonlight
& breaks yellow on black sand with the clap
of a thousand gulls being thrown up from the earth
& I sat hunched like a gutted crab in the burning salt spray
under a sky that hangs so low the lights of heaven
pressed on my head like a jeweled crown & all night
the human cry of gulls who suddenly break open their wings
& drop at fish heads flashing gold in foam & the black sun
splitting the dawn sky like an ax through hard wood
tossing splinters of flame across the horizon's fiery edge
& I rolled with the roll of the earth against water
everywhere returning the gift of light to light.

How, for a moment, a blink of time,
the whole world seemed lit from within
with a music that was fire, air, earth & water,
the gift of which, like the spines of grass he lies under,
sings & threads the wind.

Like Wings

For Marie

Last night I dreamed I was the first man to love a woman
& woke shaking & went outside to watch
the faded rag of the sky burn into dawn.
I am tired of the river before feeling,
the joy we must carve from shadow,
tired of my road-thick tongue.

I cannot hand you my breath or wrap the horizon
round your wrist & be forgiven.
I cannot rub the dry wood of my ribs to fire
& sleep. The edge of sleep isn't sleep.
I go room to room tying my feelings into knots.
The space we filled now fills me.
The light & dark won't mix.

I cannot leave myself like a house frozen in the background.
I am this body & the weather all year round.
I think of the light that opened over you our first morning,
how the glass in my lungs turned to sound
& I saw you woman & child & couldn't breathe, for love.
Fear is the edge that is the risk that is loving.
It stinks of blood, draws sharks.

The nights you waltzed naked round our bed,
myself holding the chair I'd painted blue again,
the cats flowing in the wings of your good yellow hair.
There is much men don't know about women,
how your hands work the air to water, the seed to life,
why the salt at the tips of your breasts glows
& tastes of mollusk.

There are hours when the future gives up all hope
& stops in the middle of busy streets
& doesn't care. But think of the distance we have come,
the hands which have wound us.
There will be others.

I have read of ancient people
who held razors to their doctor's throat
as he operated—as if love could have such balance,
like wings.

One night I followed your tracks through deep snow
& stood in an old schoolhouse watching the new sun
come red & shimmer over the opening fields,
the world white & flat & a light
I'd known all my life burned in my head like a fist of rags,
how I couldn't remember what we feared
we'd taken or left,
my arms opened to your shape, how I couldn't lift
out of my body, my mouth frozen
round the sound of your name.

For My Father

Samuel Schultz, 1903–1963

Spring we went into the heat of lilacs
& his black eyes got big as onions & his fat lower lip
hung like a bumper & he'd rub his chin's hard fur on my cheek
& tell stories: he first saw America from his father's arms
& his father said here he could have anything if he wanted it
with all his life & he boiled soap in his backyard & sold it door to door
& invented clothespins shaped like fingers & cigarette lighters
that played *Stars & Stripes* when the lid snapped open.

Mornings he lugged candy into factories
& his vending machines turned peanuts into pennies
my mother counted on the kitchen table & nights he came home
tripping on his laces & fell asleep over dinner & one night
he carried me outside & said only God knew what God had up His sleeve
& a man only knew what he wanted & he wanted a big white house
with a porch so high he could see all the way back to Russia
& the black moon turned on the axis of his eye & his breath
filled the red summer air with the whisky of first light.

The morning his heart stopped I borrowed money to bury him
& his eyes still look at me out of mirrors & I hear him kicking
the coal burner to life & can taste the peanut salt on his hands
& his advice on lifting heavy boxes helps with the books I lug town to town
& I still count thunder's distance in heartbeats as he taught me & one day
I watched the sun's great rose open over the ocean as I swayed on the bow
of the Staten Island Ferry & I was his father's age when he arrived
with one borrowed suit & such appetite for invention & the bridges
were mountains & the buildings gold & the sky lifted backward
like a dancer & her red hair fanning the horizon & my eyes burning
in a thousand windows & the whole Atlantic breaking at my feet.

Deep Within the Ravine

1984

Ode to Desire

Remember how we watched a hang-glider lift himself
between heaven & earth & the music in the sway
of his arms & how for a moment he was one with the light
& as perfect as the world allows — as if love were a kind
of weather where one moment there is a calm so complete
the earth rolls on its side like a woman turning
in the generous folds of her sleep & then thunder
strikes like the despair of total embrace?

Remember the newsreels of marathon dancers,
how they cling like shadows long after the music
of first passion, how they push & drag each other
like swimmers stretching toward the surface light
of their desire to continue the embrace
another quarter turn round the speckled floor?

To think that after we have given up all hope
of perfection I am still jealous of the red towel
you wrap round your raisin hair & of the photos
of you as a child who looked happy enough not to know me
& that I still cannot understand the blood's rush to give all
& the urgency that opens in my chest like an umbrella
which will not close until you take me back
into the tides of your breath!

What rage, our bodies twisted like wires
in the brain's switchboard, hurt plugged to joy,
need to desire, how it happens so quickly, this entering
of another's soul, like molecules of fire connecting
flesh & dream in the sheets of a hundred beds, spring
suddenly knocking at the window as your long female body
sprawls into full radiance, ah, such high laughter
in light-flushed rooms, our bodies so perfectly crossed!

Remember the night we read how the female whale whips
her tail out of reach as the male splits the ocean
plunging round her for whole days & nights crying
such symphony of rage birds whirl round their spindrift waltz
as the sea is shaken like a fishbowl & the sky is shredded
into ribbons of light? Yes, it is curious, the risk of such
attraction, but isn't there implanted in the anemones of her eyes
the smallest smile? — for all creatures large & small must realize
that in stirring such passion the prize must be worth the promise
& yes, I am tired of this endless dancing in circles & suddenly
the light of this spring morning does not throw back its color
so splendidly as before though there is still the joy that comes
only after long pain as you slip slowly within reach & everywhere
the air burns like the stained glass in the attic window
where I sat as a boy listening to the wind with such longing
the light itself was song!

The View

Remember how the door in our first apartment always stuck?
Now the building is a Chinese laundry & the Spaniard,
who kept us up clapping flamenco, asked where you were.

I admitted I didn't know. Perhaps too much happens
& the loss is finally for something that never existed?
Returning may be a step forward, but now the question

is how much we can bear to question. Change, I think,
happens almost always too late. Yes, I still miss
the way you washed your hands before undressing & how

your green eyes darkened with desire. I remember
what was promised. That once I believed I could die of love.
That, like fate & youth & weather, it continued forever.

This is the first day of the new year & around me everywhere
the light is less convincing. I mean to say the view this morning
from every direction is still lovely, if a little darker.

I'm Not Complaining

It isn't as if I never enjoyed good wine
or walked along the Hudson in moonlight,
I have poignant friends & a decent job,
I read good books even if they're about
miserable people but who's perfectly happy,
I didn't go hungry as a kid & I'm not constantly
oppressed by fascists, what if my apartment
never recovered from its ferocious beating,
no one ever said city life was easy, I admit
my hands turn to cardboard during lovemaking
& I often sweat through two wool blankets—
but anxiety is good for weight loss, listen,
who isn't frightened of late night humming
in the walls, I don't live in a police state,
I own a passport & can travel even if I can't
afford to, almost everyone is insulted daily,
what if love is a sentence to hard labor &
last year I couldn't pay my taxes, I didn't
go to prison, yes, I've lost friends to alcohol
& cancer but life is an adventure & I enjoy
meeting new people, sure it's hard getting older
& mysteriously shorter but insomnia & depression
afflict even the rich & famous, okay, my folks
were stingy with affection & my pets didn't live long,
believe me, sympathy isn't what I'm after, I'm basically
almost happy, God in all His wisdom knows that at heart
I'm really not complaining . . .

Mrs. Applebaum's Sunday Dance Class

Her red pump tapping, ankle-length gown slit at the knee,
Mrs. Applebaum lined us up as her husband tuned his piano,
his bald head shining under the Temple's big bay windows.
I can see it all again, the girls' shy smiles, the boys' faces
scrubbed bright as strawberries, 200 fingers anticipating trouble,
the bowing & curtsying rehearsed to a nervous perfection
by Mrs. Applebaum's High German class — it isn't hard to envision
Sarah Rosen, her bourbon curls tied in a ponytail, stepping forward
like an infant swan to choose that clod Charlie Krieger
while smiling at me! Call it first intimation of splendor,
or darker knowledge, but can't you see us, twenty dwarfs
colliding Sunday after Sunday, until, miraculously, a flourish here,
a pivot there, suddenly Davie Stern dipping Suzie Fein
to Mrs. Applebaum's shrill "Und vonce agunn, voys und gurdles!"

Oh Mrs. Applebaum, who could've guessed our wild shoving
would be the start of so much furor? You must've known
there was more to come when our lavish stretching left us dizzy,
clumsy with desire? Weren't you, our first teacher, thinking
of the day when such passion would finally take our teeth & hair?
What really channeled such light into your eyes & swayed
your powerful bosom with such force? What pushed Mr. Applebaum,
never a prize winner, to such heights? Ah Mrs. Applebaum,
didn't you notice how I sighed when Sarah didn't change partners
& stayed in my arms? I'm speaking of that terrible excess,
not the edging back, but the overflowing of all that color
flowering in our cheeks! Please, Mrs. Applebaum, remember
Sarah in pink chiffon foxtrotting, her head back & braced teeth
pressed against all that which was to come — the world of such
profound promise! Yes, remember Sarah, her eyes, for so few moments,
so blue the room everywhere around us filled with light!

My Smile

My smile won my mother trips to Niagara Falls
three years running, my black-eyed I'll-eat-
the-world-for-you twinkle of unabashed lechery
beat out every other five-year-old in Rochester, N.Y.
In one photo I'm folded artfully on a counter, my arms
twisted over my suspendered little chest like straps
in a straightjacket from which I'm struggling to burst free
like a pintsized Houdini. The suspenders alone are a stroke
of genius. My mother understood the appeal of a small boy
eager to please the female world with a wistful imitation
of masculine bravura. She knew the dark light in my eyes
came straight from the reptilian brain which owns only
one instinct: delight. Her point was appetite. You see,
I was her second chance to dazzle the world with a fire
unlike anyone else's so she fanned mine with stories
of Attila the Hun & Madame Bovary & warned me against
hiding inside bells like Quasimodo whose shyness
was uglier than his face. She herself wanted to burst open
like a poppy seed but was too frightened to reveal her brilliance.
Believe me, neither of us had much choice. My smile became
a fossil souvenir of her own desire which Quasimodo would understand.
His smile also meant business. Listen, I could go on forever about this
& with any luck, I will.

Pumpernickel

Monday mornings Grandma rose an hour early to make rye,
onion & challah, but it was pumpernickel she broke her hands for,
pumpernickel that demanded cornmeal, ripe caraway, mashed potatoes
& several Old Testament stories about patience & fortitude & for
which she cursed in five languages if it didn't pop out fat
as an apple-cheeked peasant bride. But bread, after all,
is only bread & who has time to fuss all day & end up
with a dead heart if it flops? Why bother? I'll tell you why.
For the moment when the steam curls off the black crust like a strip
of pure sunlight & the hard oily flesh breaks open like a poem
pulling out of its own stubborn complexity a single glistening truth
& who can help but wonder at the mystery of the human heart when you
hold a slice up to the light in all its absurd splendor & I tell you
we must risk everything for the raw recipe of our passion.

For My Mother

The hand of peace you sent from Israel
hangs on my wall like an ironic testament
to the one quality we have never shared.
I imagine you peering into that ancient vista
as if discovering God in the brilliant sunlight,
worrying no doubt about your bunions & weak ankles.
These words have been a long time in coming.
Once I wrote only to the dead but grief has an end.
The living are more demanding. I have seen the scar
big as a zipper on your belly where they cut you open
& ripped out six pounds of hunger demanding to be adored.
You named me Big Mouth, Big Pain, Big Wanting. Sons,
you said, suck a woman dry & leave for someone
with stronger ankles & a back better suited
to their talent for self-eulogy. Yes, men
are more selfish. Nothing demands of us
so absolute a generosity. But I have given up
the umbilicus of rage which for so long has fed me.
Now I understand why you paste every scrap of my existence
in a black book like a certificate of blood, but achievement
is not redemption & even now I cannot hold a woman
without fearing she might take too much of me. Perhaps
this is why I love a woman most during her time
when the earth is lush within her & her embrace
gives forth such privilege my passion for distance
becomes a cry for forgiveness, a desire to return
always to the beginning. No, I have not forgotten
the Saturday afternoons in movie houses when you
cried so softly I imagined I was to blame.
I remember those long walks home,
our hands a binding of such unbreakable vengeance
I can still taste the cool blue wafers of your eyes.

Believe me, there was nothing I would not have given,
nothing I would not have done for you. Remember our game
when I held your leg so tightly you had to drag me
like a ball & chain around our unhappy house? Neither of us
understood that the grip of consanguinity is nothing less
than an embrace with time. Mother, though I cannot unhinge
all this lasting sorrow or make your flesh sing, cannot
return the gift of such remarkable expansion, I am always
thinking: This is for you, this word, this breath, this tiny light,
this, my hand of peace, this wound which does not heal.

Balance

Eight years gone & the welfare building is a parking ramp.
The attendant can't recall where it went. Uptown somewhere, he thinks.
But ten thousand people filled those halls & only the ocean
is a carpet big enough to sweep so many under.

I was a clerk who read Chekhov & knew the fate of clerks.
I learned to sway down halls like a dancer & never stop to listen.
Mornings I filed dental reports & wore earplugs against the crying
for crutches, steel hands & mattresses fitted to broken backs.

A Mrs. Montvale perched on my desk & swore she'd kill herself
if her new dentures didn't arrive by Thanksgiving.
A fatalist with rotting gums, she feared dying toothless at a feast.
Near closing time the ghosts lined up around the block, still waiting.

In Central Index I watched the hundred Ferris wheels
flip rainbow cards sorting the dead from the quickly dying
& filed the electric buzz of computers into a symphony so grand
it washed the curdled voices from my head.

I'm glad the building's gone. Despair can't be tolerated
in such numbers & Gray's *Anatomy* doesn't explain
how the human body breaks a hundred ways each day & still finds balance.
Lord of Mercy, the dead still need bus fare & salvation!

Guide to the Perplexed

Maimonides believed despair was a luxury
of good intentions gone bad & that nobody
had it worse than twelfth-century Jews who
married their misery & sired whole tribes
of woe-ridden supplicants but I wonder
if he ever received mail asking him to
reserve burial space in a veterans' cemetery
when his 4-F during the last war was a
matter of record or if the Committee for
an Extended Lifespan demanded he know why
others outlived him by at least 30 years
(did he smoke, drink, eat raw flesh or
engage in deviant sexual-religious practices?)
or if his congressman harassed him to support
a bill against abortion, implying he murdered
his own kind or if his dreams replayed nightly
a pornographic commedia dell'arte in which
his woman left him for someone who sold
penis enlargers to aging bureaucrats or if
strangers called at all hours insisting
his number was listed in the S&M Newsletter
& if he was invited annually to a benefit
sponsoring the World's End—yes, he believed
in forced recognitions & diplomacy (doctoring
his enemies, he buttered both sides of every
psyche) but even Spinoza found him perplexing
(in fairness Spinoza found everyone confusing)
& often a faith's best defender is also its
worst enemy but what good really is his
fancy system for spiritual ecstasy when death
comes early in dishonorable graves while a
generation of unborn souls curse our memory

in cataracts of junk mail—did he ever weary
of Nature's magic show & desire only to lie
on his brown couch, sighing so profoundly
each rib snapped like a violin string—ah,
Maimonides, I know the twentieth century is through
(friends call to remind me) & the latest history
of our time is entitled *Vanity, Greed, Intolerance
& 30 Days to Thinner Thighs,* but am I responsible
for every abomination east of the China Sea—
Vietnam wasn't my fault & I'm not capable of
inflating the National Deficit!—Rabbi,
I realize 6,000 years of impacted grief & guilt
cannot be deducted from our taxes, but the real
question remains: What happened between your time
& mine that delivered us into the hands of
modern Manhattan?

Fifth Avenue in Early Spring

We are admiring Bergdorf's summer fashions,
myself & this young couple who coo & flutter

like cockatoos rife with seasonal pleasure.
The girl dreams aloud about moonlit beaches

while the boy, who obviously adores her,
smiles as if to share the elegance

of her long black hair which lifts like mist
curling off the nearby East River. Yes,

she is lovely, balanced on her toes
like a dancer & I doubt if she

is even thinking about returning
to South Bend or Poughkeepsie

now that we have all survived
another winter in this city

where one earns his papers slowly
& even the satisfactions can be disturbing.

But this is a night when everyone is wistful,
here on a street unlike any other,

where even those of us who are no longer
particularly innocent

are suddenly happy
to bear witness.

The Music

There is music in the spheres of the body.
I mean the pull of the sea in the blood
of the man alone on his porch watching
the stars wind bands of light around his body.
I mean the roll of the planet that is the rhythm
of his breath & the wilderness of his perception
that is the immensity of light flowering like stars
in the lights of his eyes. I mean the singing
in his body that is the world of the moment of his life,
Lord!

Lines to a Jewish Cossack:
For Isaac Babel

As a boy I cut his photo from my copy of *Red Cavalry*
& twisted my face to look properly disturbed with vision.
But irony is impossible to imitate & certainly there's
too much amused spirit in his smile though poor output
was the reason he was sent to a writer's camp, which,
let's admit, is a fate fancy enough to end one of his own stories.
Writers aren't often killed for their silence.

Yes, he loved truth too much & politics too little
to be trustworthy in the affairs of state but I think
disappointment is the spice behind the irony in his eyes.
He saw his father on his knees before a mounted Cossack captain
& disgrace is a legacy a son cannot easily forgive.
We have this in common. My father died broken of purse & spirit
& failure is a demeaning debt. I admit my own production isn't
so hot this year—I too fear being sent away.

Once he wrote that a story wasn't finished
until every line he loved most was omitted.
Yes, but the human spirit cannot withstand such revision
& we write to undo the wrong we cannot alter in our lives.

I understand that paradox makes each day
one wink or swallow less absurd & that death,
like self-loathing, can be an engaging companion,
but why would a bespectacled Jewish kid with plump cheeks
& a mind suited to Talmudic study ride with the Philistines
of his age, carrying an unloaded gun into battle—
why husband his own enemies, why such a thing?

On this spring morning it's sweet to imagine us
sipping vodka on the cusp of the Black Sea
like old friends who remain indigenous only
to that pit of ashes we call memory. What if I grew up
on Lake Ontario & am more Baltic in composition—
we share the same ironic disposition as we sit here watching
the good southern light lace our sea with such fine affection,
while swapping stories we must not understand too quickly
lest we lose their mystery, which, like grief & belly-laughter,
must last us at least another century or two.

My Guardian Angel Stein

In our house every floor was a wailing wall
& each sideward glance a history of insult.
Nightly Grandma bolted the doors believing God

had a personal grievance to settle on our heads.
Not Atreus exactly but we had furies (Uncle Jake
banged the tables demanding respect from fate) & enough

outrage to impress Aristotle with the prophetic unity
of our misfortune. No wonder I hid behind the sofa sketching
demons to identify the faces in my dreams & stayed under

bath water until my lungs split like pomegranate seeds.
Stein arrived one New Year's Eve fresh from a salvation in Budapest.
Nothing in his 6,000 years prepared him for our nightly bacchanal

of immigrant indignity except his stint in the Hundred Years' War
where he lost his eyesight & faith both. This myopic angel knew
everything about calamity (he taught King David the art of hubris

& Moses the price of fame) & quoted Dante to prove others
had it worse. On winter nights we memorized the Dead Sea Scrolls
until I could sleep without a night light & he explained why

the stars appear only at night ("Insomniacs, they study the Torah
all day!"). Once I asked him outright: "Stein, why is our house
so unhappy?" Adjusting his rimless glasses, he said: "Boychick,

life is a comedy salted with despair. All humans are disappointed.
Laugh yourself to sleep each night & with luck, pluck & credit cards
you'll beat them at their own game. Catharsis is necessary in this house!"

Ah, Stein, bless your outsized wings & balding pate & while I'm at it
why not bless the imagination's lonely fray with time, which, yes,
like love & family romance, has neither beginning, middle nor end.

In Exile

Dante wrote his wife, Gemma, about his garden
which grew double-breasted roses & plum trees,
but this was in Ravenna, where he lived in exile
for twenty years. It's enough to say he knew something
about hell, but exile is a strange business & memory
is a kind of hell & longing, too. Which reminds me
of my uncle Jake who worked in a movie house watching
the same films like one of Dante's sinners replaying
the same crime. Each night he listened to his police radio
in his room off our kitchen & wrote letters to editors
about busted traffic lights & birds starving to death.
When he died I found fifteen shopping bags full of girlie books
& badly rhymed poems about loneliness & unregenerate love.
Dante came out of his room once in a while. He understood
passion & divine punishment & knew there was more to passion
than everlasting fire. Where in his kingdom of the damned
would Jake fit? Jake, who crouched behind his bureau,
rubbing at himself like the sinners Dante placed in a pit,
each damned to gnaw the other's head for eternity. But
their punishment amplified their lives. There's transcendence
in such agony. But there was nothing metaphysical about Jake,
who sat hunched on his perch beside the screen, imprisoned
in his blasphemous fantasy & rage. Ah, Jake, a man who cannot love
is forever exiled from himself. His life is his punishment.
Think of Dante alone in his garden where the starry skies
lit up in realms of fire, music & light. Think of him scribbling
his remorseful visions all night, longing for Florence, for Gemma.
In his every word there is the pain of celebration. Yes, beauty lost
is still splendid in its reinvention. But what about Jake,
whose shoes didn't fit & who cut himself shaving every morning—
Jake, for whom there is no music of the spheres or the forgiveness
of light & who will never again behold the cold passion of the stars.

Ode

Grandma stuffed her fur coat into the icebox.
God Himself couldn't convince her it wasn't a closet.
"God take me away this minute!" was her favorite Friday night prayer.
Nothing made sense, she said. Expect heartburn & bad teeth, not sense.
Leave a meat fork in a dairy dish & she'd break the dish & bury the fork.
"I spit on this house, on this earth & on God for putting me
in this life that spits on me night & day," she cried, forgetting the barley
in barley soup. It wasn't age. She believed she was put here to make
one unforgivable mistake after another. Thou shalt be disappointed
was God's first law. Her last words were: "Turn off the stove
before the house blows up." Listen, I'm thirty-four already
& nothing I do is done well enough. But what if disappointment
is faith & not fate? What if we never wanted anything enough to hurt over?
All I can say is spring came this year with such a wallop
the trees are still shaking. Grandma, what do we want from them?
What do we want?

Personal History

My father is playing solitaire in the last train compartment.
He turns over a card named The End of the Journey Is Grief.
He is after God, the conductor says, taking our unmarked tickets.

My mother stands at the end of the corridor, frozen in her silence
like a fly seized in amber. The train passes the house where I was born
& the wheel in my chest slaps my ribs awake. I wave at myself (the boy

in the attic window) but cannot hear what I am crying as we pass
the cemetery where all our personal history is buried. You will be
remembered only in the dark dreams of strangers, the conductor sings.

Yes, but faith isn't allowed in our century, my mother answers.
We are all born in exile, my father says, turning over a card named
Diaspora. Yes, it has been that all along, I think, holding my own hand.

My mother anoints me with the brilliant glass of her disaffection
as we all stare out the window into the dark where the stars continue
to survive like syllables of an extinct but beautiful language.

The Quality

There is in each body something splendid, I think,
    a kind of sheltering, say, the suit of
hours we wear like weather, or instinct striking
    the spine's cold accordion, that ripening
of reflex that is the mind's appetite for testimony,
    yes, in darkness there is strength hoarded

against damage, say, the flowering of desire imprinted
    in the infant's smile as it awakens out of
its dream of creation, I mean pain is not sentiment only,
    but a fierce healing, like light rebuilding,
out of darkness, our original boundaries, yet something
    is lost in the growing, yes, the greater

the gift the more troubling the sleep, like lovers lost
    in the body's cold spin, we are naked
within the shell of our temperament, beings greater in
    mystery after violation, yes, like strips
of horizon, the spirit unwinds its gift of a single life,
    moment by moment, say, that quality of love

that is not physical, but sensed, like vision burning
    in the eye's garden, yes, once again spring
arrives after winter's long ash & I accept despair's
    selfish fruit as the fermenting of wonder
that springs out of everything lost & dying, say,
    that furthering of instinct, which, like

the spider's ambition to infinitely extend its life
    another inch of light, glistens like rain
over the attic window where I sat as a boy entranced
    with the radiance of first longing, yes,
a quality so distinctly human we glow like light burning
    over all the fire-struck windows of our lives.

FROM

The Holy Worm of Praise

2002

The Holy Worm of Praise

To my friends on my fiftieth birthday

Let's raise our glasses and give thanks
to our great excitement and hunger
for the hereafter the joyful sleep
of expectation the Pentecostal suffering
that seizes entire winter afternoons in amber
our best days that shake us with fear and envy
our nights of provocative kissing
behind hotel rhododendrons
the secret lives we cannot remember
the deathbeds we visit like locusts
like holy scripture the fragile façade
of our psyche and its ricocheting runways
our appetite for remorse and belly-laughter and Kafka
our Knights of Infinite Resignation
our merciless opinions and monotonous disappointments
which fill our mouths with ash and feathers
our successes which beat us unconscious
demanding homage and impeccable manners
the white noise of self-loathing
and boomerang of self-pity
our kowtowing and bootlicking and toad-eating
the propitious future of our unforgiving past
our quoting Descartes without thinking
our pockets filled with blasphemy and fluster
our enemies who find us original and therefore hateful
our stuttering like Moses whom God entrusted
with so many important messages
the mistakes we mistook for privilege
the allegiance pledged to satisfaction
the delusion framed and hung over mantles
the illegitimate ideas abandoned on roadsides
our gargling garlic and hot ginger while drifting

down the Lethe of rainy Sundays
our eulogizing memories of tranquillity
and hoarding apples of discord
our ontological orgies and losing
of couth in games of quoit our prophecies
scribbled on napkins in differential equations
our Nijinsky leaping off the tongue's springboard
our Talmudic rapture and musical pajamas
our brass candlesticks gleaming like Statues of Liberty
our circular journey to singular moments
the organ crescendos of our lies and promises
our crawling dubitably along godless lifelines
our daily umbrage and masticating jaws and death row memoirs
our Euclidean fornication and obsessive sucking
our forgiving no one anything
our hands trembling like trophies of prophetic plunder
our hair breasts and genitals adorned with salutations
our rhythmic breathing and sphinxlike smiling
our being yanked headfirst out of kindness
our emigrant embarking our forty years
of wandering in the present moment
our fifty years of looking for it
our indomitable gardens
our craving constant illumination
the halos of our eyes mouths nipples and anuses
the holy worm of our tongues singing praise
our faces shining like cities our being one among many
our climbing Jacob's ladder to rock in the arms of angels
our walking here and there on the earth and looking around

Courtship According to My Guardian Angel Stein

Tradition demands that the hand you kiss
shouldn't tighten into a fist, but never try to
make nice when she's washing venetian blinds
or talk about old loves when she's drinking wine.
Schopenhauer said a woman by nature is meant to obey
but he also wrote at great length about suicide
and don't even think about removing her nightgown
after her mother phones. A pretty face doesn't make
for a good wife, a crooked foot is better than a crooked mind
and everyone knows courtship begins after marriage
and continues into death and if it seems you can do
nothing right it may be what she likes about you most.
If she says no one will love you half as much tell her
half a story is a story nonetheless. After the wedding
it's too late for regrets and everything ends with weeping.
In other words: Man thinks and God laughs and shrouds
are made without pockets. Be grateful for a home.

Flying Dogs

In early spring color pokes its chilly nose through the earth
reminiscing about past hibernations with ocean winds
inflating the sky one billowing cloud at a time and trees shed
metaphysical shadows that drift lazily along the river
known for its sexual boasting while brownstones rub
against tenements like cats unfurling in windows —
but it's the dogs who are flying! Gus, our smooth Fox Terrier,
rises on white and brown spotted wings while Benya, our black Lab mix,
loop-the-loops on powerful hawk wings, both gliding over rooftops
scaring up flocks of pigeons as neighbors climb onto fire escapes
to watch them nosedive and whirl high over Charles Street. Dylan
the cross-eyed Dalmatian is up there with Betsy the Saluki and Ruggles
the Chow Chow, who smells like Quasimodo, is double-dipping Matty
the ballbrain Irish Setter who'd go to Mars to fetch, and there's Hector
the submissive Whippet and his girlfriend, Tulip, the pertinacious Pekinese,
whooping it up with Sir Quintin the operatic Golden who's howling
something Verdi high over Sheridan Square. Yes, it's spectacular:
Giant Schnauzers, somersaulting Newfoundlands and Portuguese Water Dogs
bounding over Great Pyrenees, who can boogie-woogie with the best,
Bearded Collies, benighted Dobermans and happy-go-lucky Akitas,
forlorn Bull-mastiffs, beset Rhodesians, bandy Malamutes and Pharaoh Hounds
flying around water towers high over celebratory bridges stretching from one
surprising moment to another in this city where I lived deep in winter long
before I met you or imagined a smile so beguiling light would thaw
and the horizon vibrate like a violin string.

On First Hearing of Your Conception

Premature no doubt, my heading north
through the kitchen to the dining room
which is south but also west depending on
whether one is going forward to the future
or backward toward the middle of what
used to be my life in the shadows of the
living room which is now a place you will
pass through on your way to grander things.
Indeed, one must ponder the importance of
this autumn light which seems more robust
in each window. Yes, I'm walking in circles
while your mother reads about the drama
of evolution which took its time building
toward its denouement from amoebae to
somersaulting the hectic surf of our most
epic journey. Weigh each drip of gravity,
lift the tiny idea of your arms, defy the odds,
evolve.

The Monologue

I lived in a monologue a long time.
It rambled on about people it impressed,
work it had done, prizes it had won.
It remembered every insult. Agreed
with no one. Mourned the living
and sanctified the dead. Insisted
it knew what was best for me.
Whispered in my ear like a lover
who didn't know my name.
The past was its domain.
Forgive no one, it said. Abstain.
Inherit the kingdom of death.

Sick

Every Wednesday morning for one year
I volunteered in an outpatient ward
for children too angry for public school.
Ten- to fifteen-year-olds, they wrote about
mothers who boiled their hands to scare
the devil away, trying to scrape the blackness
off their face, fishing for cats on fire escapes
and fornicating in alleyways, why despair
tasted like leather and smelled like smoke —
until a doctor said: Stop coming, these kids
are too sick for poetry. On our last morning
I played the fool (as they liked me to: "White guy
goin' to fat, no hair to slick, who's he kiddin'
comin' so far uptown, playin' wit' the downs
an' outs . . ."), singing about a nightingale.
The poet was dying, I said, but he wrote
about visions and faery lands. About beauty.
About hope. I said, Please, taste the truth
in each syllable, but their eyes stayed dead
and I left feeling I might've helped them
if I had tried a little harder.

The Inside and The Outside

The outside is bigger,
especially at night
when you turn the lights on,
there it is,
surrounding everything,
not worrying.
This drives the inside crazy,
makes it want to go further inside
until it has become its own outside
until it expects nothing.
It likes to stand at its window
looking at the outside
being so pleased with itself,
with what it has evolved into
without any help from anyone,
not even those of us who go
from one to the other
not knowing exactly
where we are.

The Answering Machine

They don't counterfeit enthusiasm by raising their volume
or use static to suggest disdain or indignation. They don't
hold grudges and aren't judgmental. They're never too busy
or bored or self-absorbed. They possess a tolerance for isolation
and conscience and always remember who's calling. Cowardice
is permitted, if enunciated clearly. I broke off with Betsy by
telling her machine I couldn't go rafting with her in Colorado.
I meant *anywhere* and it understood perfectly. They appreciate
how much intimacy we can bear on a daily basis. When one becomes
overburdened it buries all pertinent information by overlapping.
Whatever happened, say, to Jane's sweet birthday song, hidden
under so many felicitations about my appendix operation, or Bill's
news of his father's death preempted by Helen's wedding invitation?
All these supplanted voices are a constant reminder of everything
we promised and forgot, the plaintive vowels and combative consonants
rubbing into a piercing vibrato of prayerlike insistence. Everything
we feared to say or mean; our very silence . . . an ongoing testimony
which we replay nightly and then erase to make room for more . . .

Ars Poetica

Here we are on a reading circuit somewhere East of Eden,
in a Comfort Inn watching *The Magnificent Seven*, again,
anticipating a roomful of Dickensians, one of whom fingers
1,000 rhyming pages on Jack the Ripper's unrequited love
for Moll Flanders's stuffed parrot, Rosy, that he'd like you
to glance at. Yesterday you drove 100 rainy miles to an Elks
convention, four furry heads bobbing on a sea of Seagram's,
two snoring before you began your crowd-warmer Elegies
to Depression, a third keeping time coughing while the fourth
wept uncontrollably because his horse, Polygamy, died
17 years ago that very night and you looked a little like him.
Then the Eliot experts rushed you through dinner after your plane
circled Nirvana for hours and you grabbed a leatherbound winelist
instead of your manuscript and found yourself in a church spotlight
under a swaying crucifix, staring at a list of Zinfandels with 400 feet
tapping, your sponsors wishing you'd come and gone like the women
talking of Michelangelo . . . well, soon it'll be morning and only one
Magnificent will have survived while another of the 66 people
who buy poetry books will have died and no, you don't get nosebleeds
while reading publicly anymore but, after all these years, you're still
cranking up waxed wings for one more nutsy flight, always looking
for that one smiling face that loves you unconditionally . . .

Personally

I didn't fight for my country, Vietnam came and went
while I continued washing my face as if nothing happened.
What happened, exactly? All those trick questions in school
about history, me dreaming about the Warsaw Ghetto,
heroes of the French Revolution screaming freedom, equality!
The heroes in my neighborhood made doughnuts and gaskets,
felt their way around the dark without enough information.
Information is crucial, like satisfaction. But what is it, exactly?
Does anyone feel important, really? Even the big oaks we kept stabbing
—why did we hate them? They were bursting with strength and freedom,
watching us come and go like so much traffic. Every day now
something darkens, becomes less familiar, more distant. Know the feeling?
Actually, there's no feeling. Only appetite. Weather surrounding everything,
dark, wet, indifferent. I used to hide in the dirt cellar looking at Dad's boxes
of failed ideas. Like him, I take things personally, turn lights off, tighten things.
I ducked the draft, hid in fear and righteousness. The Berlin Wall went up
and came down again amid all that dust and yelling about freedom, the point is
something *happening* . . . getting a good seat at the Zeitgeist. Oaks know
equality isn't about satisfaction, but failure . . . like Dad's idea for cars to run
on Epsom salt, it didn't work but one wants to make a contribution,
be part of things, a citizen of one's sweet little slice of history . . .

Prison Doctor

I fix every kind of stab wound, fractured clavicle,
gold teeth sliced out of sleeping mouths for trophy
earrings, all paranoia's graffiti pleading Doc please
yank this sardine-can shaft, this mea culpa, out of
my memory. I don't perform haruspical inspection,
the nasty custom, but we're all Etruscans here,
apostates suffering hallucinatory visions, exiled
from the future, fleeing God's imagination. What
Heidegger said: saying a thing brings it into being
exists here in reverse where thinking makes things
disappear: Sundays, weather, a spring afternoon
on the verandah, faith, a glimpse of infinity . . . Outside
everyone is human a few hours a week, loves caveats,
explanations, identifying aspects of reality; here, time
dominates, promulgates extraordinary instincts, loves
unforgivable mistakes. I too suffer night sweats, own
curtained eyes, a persona scrubbed clean of delusion.
Sleep in a windowless room, a night screamer. Mother
was a physician, her father and grandfather all healers,
back when Main Street wasn't yet Wall Street. I came
of my own volition, believing this was the last honest place.
The truth is: I *was* already a prisoner; divided not by idea,
religion or geography, but fear of what lived in my soul's
basement. I refused to suffer the world, felt only the power
of status. Here, everyone suffers pride but status is tolerance
for despair. Honor despair, its fidelity and clarity; live beside,
before and underneath your life, let your knuckles scrape, be
a profile, a tattoo of Christ kissing himself, a leper; I say:
arrive out of Egypt, be private, all-encompassing, messy.
Fashion your own tiny acre of self, atone; live without syntax
or wings; say: no thanks. Swallow your fate. Your need to mean
something; weep an inch deeper each night. Survive thyself.

The Dead

There are so many already. Probably
more than enough. Turn down any street
and you will see them just standing there,
waiting to be recognized. They don't mingle,
or talk. There's no news or gossip or luck.
Nothing to get used to. Or risk. Or give up.
They don't explore new neighborhoods
or notice much, preferring their own company.
They no longer have family or friends so no one
notices how little they've changed. You'll find
who you're looking for dreaming at a window,
waiting to be remembered. Anyone will do.

The Displaced

Grandma hated the Russians who attacked the Ukrainians
who tormented the Romanians who pissed on everyone's roses
and played around with everyone's wives. This was Rochester, New York,
in the fifties, when all the Displaced Persons moved in and suddenly
even the oaks looked defeated. Grandma believed they came here
so we all could suffer, that soon we'd all dress like undertakers
and march around whispering to the dead. Mr. Schwartzman hired me
to write letters nobody answered. He wrote about Mrs. Tillem's
boardinghouse, where everyone stank of sardines and spat in the sink;
about his job at the A&P providing for everyone else's appetite.
He never wrote about what'd happened to his music or family.
Saturday mornings for two years he spoke Yiddish as I wrote
my twelve-year-old English until I found him hanging in his closet
with a note pinned to his tie: "Live outwardly, objectify!" Yes, Goethe,
famous for beating hexameters on his mistress's back while lovemaking
because art was long, life was short, and the dead also didn't belong anyplace.

The Children's Memorial at Yad Vashem

For Hana Amichai

Inside a domed room photos of children's faces
turn in a candlelit dark as recorded voices
recite their names, ages and nationality.
"Ah, such beautiful faces," a woman sighs.
Yes, but faces without the prestige
of the future or the tolerance of the past.
Not one asks: Why is this happening to me?
They stare at the camera as if it were a commandment:
thou shall not bear false witness . . .

Why would anyone want to take their photo,
remember what they no longer looked like?
There's no delusion in their eyes,
no recognition or longing, only
the flatness of hours without minutes,
hunger without appetite.

They understand they are no longer children,
that death is redundant, and mundane.
Expected, like a long-awaited guest
who arrives bearing the gift
of greater anticipation. Their eyes
are heavy—fear perhaps,
or the unforgiving weight
of knowledge.

Did they understand why they were so hated?
Wonder why they were Jews?

Did God hear their prayers and write
something in one of his glistening books?

Were they of too little consequence?
What did they think of God, finally?

Dante cannot help us.
Imagination is the first child in line.
They cannot help us.
It is wrong to ask them.
Philosophy cannot help us,
nor wisdom, or time.
Or memory.

We look at their faces and their faces look at us.
They know we are pious.
They know we grieve.
But they also know we will soon leave.
We are not their mothers and fathers,
who also could not save them.

I Remember

For Yehuda Amichai

I remember walking you home so you could walk me home
so I could walk you halfway back, until, finally,
you walked one block to finish a last story like a blessing.

I remember our wandering around the Circus Maximus
of Times Square to Mozart, you proved, beating time
on my back, your hand in the crowd conducting ecstasy.

I remember the warm yogurt of the Dead Sea,
wiggling our toes and balancing the sun on our noses
like comedian seals, God, for once, speechless.

I remember the Jerusalem you showed me like a wound,
every tree, street, and shadowed doorway.
I remember the stars burning in the night like graves.

I remember our driving eight hundred miles
to move my mother into a nursing home, your kissing
her hand like a soldier saluting an act of courage.

I remember our silence at the Western Wall,
our prayers hovering in the air like hummingbirds.
I remember your smiling as if everything had been forgiven.

I remember our singing Vallejo, Tranströmer, Szymborska,
in a classroom, the joy in your hooded eyes,
the cancer scraping your blood like a scythe.

I remember your drifting off in cafés like an astronaut
turning in space, attached only by an umbilicus of faith,
the light in your eyes moving farther and farther away.

Apartment Sale

Mrs. Apple thought I wasn't looking
when she dropped my mother's gold pin
down her blouse, then snorted
after haggling me to fifteen dollars
for the cherrywood breakfront
that looked exactly like the one
Jackie Kennedy had in the White House.
Mr. Pepps decided against my father's
first get-rich scheme — a flintless lighter —
but paid fifty cents for a honeymoon mug
my mother got in Atlantic City. He himself
didn't care for marriage, but liked coffee.
My mother's best friend, Bea, got
the mother-of-pearl hairbrush she coveted,
but looked insulted. The Salvation Army
took the blue sofa with a big moon stain
rising over twenty-one ocean waves.
I kept a photo of my mother standing
at attention in front of our old house,
smiling with her eyes closed, as if
she didn't want to see everything
that was going to happen. A big bow,
pink, I imagine, in her blond curls.

Nomads

I've come to clean my mother's room out,
fit everything she owned into one handbag.
"They pick things up in one room and drop
them in another," Lisa, the head nurse, says,
explaining why my mother's wedding ring
is missing. "Dementia makes them roam,
they forget which room is theirs." I look at
a photo by my mother's bedside. "You were
a beautiful child and Lill's so young and pretty.
She'd stare at it for hours . . ." The boy looks
like me when I was three but my mother
was never slender like this woman. I wonder,
though, if she ever saw a photo of me in another
woman's room and thought I looked familiar.
I was the one thing she did right, she told me,
yet I wasn't part of the past she remembered.
"Will anyone miss this?" I ask, dropping
the photo in her bag. "No," Lisa smiles,
"nobody here misses anything."

Stories

Lillian Schultz, 1907–1998

Nights she counted coins from my father's vending machines,
stacked nickels dimes pennies into houses, neighborhoods
with streets and backyards and little boys under kitchen tables
watching their mother's feet tapping, her nails on waxy wood
splaacckkcctt splaacckkcctt until her eyes got sleepy and she
picked me up and carried me to the tub, water jumping
raauuummppphh and slid me down the steaming, her breasts
wet and soapy as she scrubbed me a plump pink chicken,
humming *lala aaa uuiieeoo laaa* and lifted me high and kissed me,
singing, My darling little man! and carried me to my room
to dry me in a big soft towel while I pretended not to like it,
twisting as she rubbed harder. Ticklish, eh! she laughed, ticklish
little rabbit, her fingers crinkly with talcum, jumping on my stomach
until I howled—Oh, I could eat you up *arruummpphh!* munching
my fingers toes, my heart kaalluummpping as she told stories
about being a girl when every yard had gardens like countries
in Europe with cherry and black plum and apple and pear trees,
her hair so long her mother braided it in pink ribbons and all
the women wore kerchiefs and bright peasant dresses waving
like flags up one street and down another smiling good morning
telling every brilliant thing their children did with one hand tied
behind their backs and all the old widows deep in windows, window
widows she called them, always complaining but everyone spoke
five languages at once and every house was white with red shutters
and she and her sister walked around flirting with boys in derbies
and every spring Saturday she helped her mother do wash in the backyard
and the splashing soaked the air and the grass glistened and everywhere
in branches cardinals and blue jays and robins singing and in winter
the snow came blowing off the lake like clouds burying the houses
and men tied colored hankies to car antennas but children switched them
so every morning the cursing and now she was laughing, her head back
as I moved closer and she put her arms around me and rocked us
and I wanted it to last forever, the two of us, together, always.

Darwin, Sweeping

It's not light yet and Dowen is out sweeping our tenement steps,
the same ones he used to paint every few months. Somehow
the color was never right. A super for forty years, everyone
on the block knows him but can't get his name right—Hey, Darwin
come fix my flood, I've been burgled, my husband beat me again,
I'm afraid of the dark. Once a girlfriend left me twice in one week
and he understood. I didn't, but he did. Hey, Darwin, is the Mayor coming?
I smile and he smiles back. Bernice, his wife of fifty-one years, died last week
and that's why he's sweeping the steps, the walk, the street too. Once
he painted our steps a shy jellyfish red, the kind you see off the islands
of the Galápagos Archipelago and overnight our building was an island
unto itself, a glimpse of infinity, a moment of discovery
on a long voyage home, part of the overall picture.

The Eight-Mile Bike Ride

In memory of John Cheever

Sundays we cranked old bikes up hills
until our legs burned and our faces glowed
and our breath twisted down winter inroads
and wind froze our hands as trees measured
the glide of seasons. Splendid was his word
for that rich winding Hudson Valley country,
the hills' swaggering color, gravel sparkling,
rain on our smiling faces, the bridge slick
with first snow, each hill a challenge of chains
whish whish the sibilance of macadam — Geronimo!
he'd yell, as we'd go headlong, hands like sails.
Once he somersaulted over handlebars and gashed
his head leaving a looping red trail eight miles long
we spotted months later. But nothing mattered,
not pain which was familiar, a kind of knowing,
like skies opening deeper into light, only trees
and weather and hills mattered, as we drifted reckless
in surrender. No one told a better story. Even
the trees listened, bending to that pure Yankee
hone of language flowing like the spicy stink
of river. The air cracked as we rode around
seasons, as in his story of the swimmer,
the light beginning in summer, fierce and dark
in windows, all those lives hurrying toward
an end which is always surprising, even
when expected. Once we stopped to watch
the night rinse through the heavens, the stars
so silent he said they looked lonely. I think
he meant to tell me that all good stories
are sad, finally, and we make such good stories,
but the window lights grow brighter, burning
with all the others as they do now in memory,
where we are splendid still, every Sunday.

The Silence

for RJ

You always called late and drunk,
your voice luxurious with pain,
I, tightly wrapped in dreaming,
listening as if to a ghost.

Tonight a friend called to say your body
was found in your apartment, where
it had lain for days. You'd lost your job,
stopped writing, saw nobody for weeks.
Your heart, he said. Drink had destroyed you.

We met in a college town, first teaching jobs,
poems flowing from a grief we enshrined
with myth and alcohol. I envied the way
women looked at you, a bear blunt with rage,
tearing through an ever-darkening wood.

Once we traded poems like photos of women
whose beauty tested God's faith. "Read this one
about how friendship among the young can't last,
it will rip your heart out of your chest!"

Once you called to say J was leaving,
the pain stuck in your throat like a razor blade.
A woman was calling me back to bed
so I said I'd call back. But I never did.

The deep forlorn smell of moss and pine
behind your stone house, you strumming
and singing Lorca, Vallejo, De Andrade,
as if each syllable tasted of blood,
as if you had all the time in the world . . .

You knew your angels loved you
but you also knew they would leave
someone they could not save.

The Dalai Lama

In memory of Joseph Brodsky

It was a lovely spring morning in Greenwich Village in 1981
and I was wandering about muttering to myself about my work,
a woman, the usual things, when I bumped into him . . .
Lost in thought, eh? he laughed. Indeed. Lost in too much "me" . . .
unlike him, I never stood up to an idea that stood up to me,
said good-bye to country, family, friends, everything.
Pilgrim hero in need of a haircut, he was on his way to see the Dalai Lama,
who'd summoned him! But what does one say to *the* Dalai Lama?
he asked. I said: Joseph, be yourself, once again speak up!
Wonderful advice, he yelled, I'll do just that! To this day I wonder
what they talked about, the world as we know it, or would like it to be,
or something more mystical, like the sadness of exile,
and the courage of spring . . .

To William Dickey

I was his student but he treated me like a colleague,
introduced me to Mr. Berryman, and Theodore Roethke.
The last time I saw him his hair was dyed henna, his wife
was gone, he introduced me to his boyfriend and vodka

mixed with milk, insisted I read H. Crane, Dickinson, too.
Once I called after finding my house empty. M, I said,
had left me again, as he said she would; he demanded
I toss Crane and read Basho, I needed "lightness" but only

on a full stomach. Then he sang, "That evil passed, so also
may this," quoting an anonymous poet living in exile.
The day he died I dreamed I was hurrying to his house
with a new poem, yelling, Bill, I think you'll like this one.

Sitting cross-legged on a rug in his Victorian house
high above San Francisco, we spoke in Haiku, drank vodka
mixed with milk. Smiling, he asked me to read it again,
but more slowly this time, in order to taste the music.

Stein, Good-bye

What kind of guardian angel are you,
moping at the window, wings drooping
and domed brow bent as if listening to
the sad music of the spheres? Old friend,
don't be forlorn, soon you'll be busy
recycling another recalcitrant soul back
into human circulation. Isn't it satisfying
to notch a wing under restitution? I'm not
ungrateful, I'll miss the pickled herring
on your breath, the Stetson that belonged
to Wild Bill Levi, the first Jewish cowboy,
your pacing in hallways as I labored to
deliver my first sestina, your dentures
clicking on subways, a flatulent Talmudist
seized with Solomonic wisdom. It's time
to find another soul to rescue. I'm still
bewildered, tremble with fear of judgment,
suffer my rewards and believe in rejuvenation . . .
a reluctant dancer who must keep moving,
slowly, into the future . . . Stein, good-bye.

The dark between

the starry hush
and shadowy rust
in the wallpaper's bloom

the child's sofa bed dreams
and warped room's well
in the echoing house

the collected escapes
and biblical hymns
in the whispering weeds

the long hungry weep
and suitcase shame
in the Diaspora sprawl

the scrap metal dead
and horses of rage
down kettledrum stones

the history of black sighs
and sway of great whys
in the stained glass rain

the miraculous wounds
and steerage eyes
of the enormous dead

the doing what we must
and stars diced to ice
in the boomeranging night

the nation of bells
and extravagant return
to the God no one judged

the oblivious shrug
and traveling so far
in the dark between

Mr. Parsky

1

His big monkey hands slapping shiny boxes,
singing brass gold silver handles silk-lined payment plans,
an invoiced infinity with no secrets or pockets to put them in.

My father's body stripped of its nakedness,
leaking fluorescence and the stink of embalming fluid,
his mind's peeling ember still reciting Pushkin,

kicking steaming chickens into the air between swallows,
swinging freely in every direction,
his nostril antennae vibrating with a litany of insults.

Okay, Mr. Parsky, we'll take the cheapest
least shiny worm-hungry cradle-rocking
most womanly-shaped never-waking one.

His eyes sprinkling the cold blue shock
of two hundred spring birds singing
open your chest and let the river out.

2

His black mule hauling a pickled gravity,
the gray sky jerked down like a shade,
expect rain he says, its sonorous riff

and cleansing scrape of robust decay
buried deep in the mind's honeycomb,
where all the guilt is stored.

He doesn't take my hand or say:
try not to understand anything
or: deplore sympathy

or: be deaf and dumb,
a troglodyte's black lichen eyes,
the sweet undertaste of the sublime,

nightmare served medium-rare
with brussels sprouts and wet crinkly spinach
lots of olive oil the expensive kind,

never says: enjoy the evolving leap
the high step of epic promise,
what he says is: hello and welcome.

3

My father's dreams—where are they?
Do they still stutter with exuberance,
pull dimes out of their ears,

believe they invented the hula hoop
but didn't get to the patent office in time,
argue with themselves in the basement all night,

squeeze greasy nickels out of candy machines,
cruise the heavens in a red Cadillac
singing *I'm a Yankee Doodle Dandy*?

4

Mr. Parsky says his boxes are made
of the kind of molecules they send to Mars,
the kind a worm bangs his head against

and piss can't rust, the kind
you can grow roots and be bottomless inside.
Seamless tugboats lugging spoiled cargoes

up and down the steaming Styx,
imagine, he says, stowaways
still dreaming of America.

5

The mess a father makes: piss-soaked sheets,
a face turning one hundred shades of blue,
choking on last words: oh it ain't gonna rain no more!

pockets full of salted IOUs,
coins from his peanut machines,
his one suit hanging in the closet like a suicide,

death no excuse not to work hundred-hour weeks,
bang hammer his way to Kingdom Come
and back each goddamn day.

Now no one's scared to step up
and slap dirt on his face, the same kind
he carried from Russia under his fingernails.

6

Mr. Parsky's rattle of mementos:
cracked dentures eyeglasses old keys,
the perfidy and hindsight he overhears,

last wishes and regrets, stone angels
bloated with Talmudic prophecy:
he is a garden of trompe l'oeils,

an implacable juggernaut,
Charon seeking verisimilitude,
his best suit pressed and pantless.

7

Mr. Parsky says: list his assets for a eulogy,
okay: a postcard of a prodigal landscape he ruminated in,
his conscience frozen like a slice of wedding cake,

a photo of his rabbi's lugubrious eyes,
a recording of Ezekiel singing *Mack the Knife*,
the sea smell of his wife's hair in moonlight,

a fingernail clipping shaped like a bedspring,
a covetous sigh a baby tooth stained with appetite,
an arm where a boy hangs laughing upside down.

8

Mr. Parsky swings his arms around,
imagine, he says, a glittering Transcendence
hovering like a monarch butterfly,

time's conveyor belt ticking past
like a freight car rattling the beyond,
the conductor's rouged unsmiling face nodding good-bye.

Don't ask what comes next,
the dark's an ignorant rhyme,
a spine bent into a question mark,

instead, imagine the elapsed, the gone by,
a statuesque stroll through the park,
the hunger of embryo wings.

Souls Over Harlem

There may be always a time of innocence.
There is never a place.

—WALLACE STEVENS

1

East
on the Long Island Expressway
toward Montauk, my wife and I
on the lam so to speak,
away
      from our appetite
for calumny, the bone scrape
and tongue-stropping angst
of the big Avenues, from
the bow and genuflect
and gargoyle melancholy
of subway faces reading ads
for heraldic tattoos and Chivas swank,
the Hudson's pungent breath,
the Christmas delirium tremens—
fleeing all this on a Friday night
for a respite of two days and nights
near the ocean, in East Hampton.

2

      Seeking Mozart,
my wife tunes
to a news bulletin
declaiming here's what's happening
right *now:* a black man, one Roland J. Smith, Jr.,
alias Abubunde Mulocko, has shot
and burned eight people dead,
himself included, in Freddy's Fashion Mart,
      a clothing store

on the umbilicus of 125th Street
across from the Apollo Theater,
where he vended gold teeth,
        stolen prosthetics
and Rolex pipe dreams,
it seems this Abu-bun-de Mu-lock-o
went nuts, way over the edge
of reason, for reasons lost
as my wife finds the Jupiter
Symphony no. 41.

3

        The next morning
in our cozy kitchen
in a quiet village
near the ocean,
I read the newspaper.
        Apparently,
it happened this way:
a black record shop, a good citizen
of 125th Street for twenty years,
was being evicted by Freddy's Fashion Mart,
owned and managed by Jews
from Queens, thus months
of *burn the Jews* homonyms
while Motown and Mingus swelled bliss
over Harlem's concrete,
and Mr. Smith, alias *Mulocko*,
feeling his soul was being evicted too,
stepped into Freddy's as the chosen
messenger of the Almighty's Wrath
against the infidels.

But Freddy's rented
from a black Baptist congregation,
which owned the building

and was raising Freddy's rent,
so Freddy's raised its sublet's rent,
the black record shop—which means
Abubunde could've used a story
more open to complications
than Samson and the Philistines.

4

    Zigzagging
the hydrant spray of surf,
two brilliant canines
and one aging attendant
scouting scents left some time
before Christ discovered America,
looking perhaps
      for a spume
of illusory spice, wind
and sand speckling our faces
    under morning's
violet thumbprint, Monica,
at home making blueberry pancakes
(the kind you can taste with all
your previous lives), singing
to her flowering belly,
as our three-year-old son
    sails his ancient dreamships
off our deck into
the ocean light.

5

    The radio says:
Mulocko's conscience objected
to Vietnam—"I deny my citizenship,"
he told the Antichrist judge,

"I, my people are slaves *here*,
why should we fight your war? . . ."
        Another island
refugee seeking the dream
of democracy in a cardboard box,
sweeping frying polishing
to marry a doorway,
give his name to a subway grate
to earn his keep, but
        he said no, simply
refused to go, so they wrapped
him in black and white stripes,
jailed his righteous ass, so
he could think things through
for a year or two,
understand the rules,
        God's vigilante,
chained to a prison rock
in the Bronx, an immigrant
Prometheus, hammered (I imagine)
into a rusty hinge
of rage and unrequited
sorrow.

6

        I too
objected,
refused to fight
for my country, claimed
my mind was a rhapsody
of splendid stigmata opposed
to a central governing body,
pleaded argued schemed
(until they believed me)
following in the steps of my friend R

who starved himself,
spoke in hieroglyphics,
claimed he was a living stillborn,
      until, exactly
twenty-seven years ago,
he said, okay, enough
and parked on a cliff
in the cold wind of the Pacific
and stuck his mulatto face
in a plastic bag
and drank snail poison,
and burned his intestines
to an ash transparency.

7

      That was
twenty-seven years ago,
his age when
he sold everything (piano,
books, his original jazz music,
everything)
      and moved into his VW
to ponder Camus' most important question.
In grad school he was famous
for translating Celan's *Death Fugue*,
looked good in shades,
played a cool jazz piano,
his cigarette dangling
on his lower lip (a matter of principle),
      way beyond cool,
right shoulder raised
            in a turkey trot riff,
a man breathing his life in all the way
            to the last moment.

Nights we drove his VW convertible
through the wheat fields, under
the sky's luminant houseguests,
singing Yehuda Amichai
and Osip Mandelstam,
yes, he wanted to be ancient,
a Jew like me,
while I wanted a powerful black soul,
to live deep in a parenthesis,
where, like him,
        I wouldn't need anyone.

Once he wrote:
        he was going to lock himself up in a dead man
        he was sick of the music of human beings
Once he knocked on my door in the middle of the night
and said:
        please stay away from me

8

        Deep
in the husk of her studio
Monica pulls and twists
with acetylene flame
two-inch rods
        into faces,
half human, half beast,
heads on sticks she calls them,
cold steel transmogrified
into souls that howl deep
in our backyard under
the moon's fluorescence,
form elongated into dream
by her strong hands—

"The Family,"
she calls them, fallen angels,
happy (I think)
to have found fertile soil
    among our maples
and sycamores and wild roses,
blooming in winter, deep
in the mind's manure — yes,
a family, no different,
finally, from any other.

9

    Tonight,
in bed, Monica remembers
her mother's argument
with memory (whether
her mother's cattle car had a stove,
she recalls something burning)—
I say, of course the mind
demands a stove, only so
much reality can be sustained
before the mind disappears
inside its dreams. I think,
of course Abubunde Mulocko
owned an argument, a stove
he couldn't forgive,
no doubt he hung out,
jived with stones,
plucked
    a few devious strings,
wore an earring in his nose ear eyebrow,
drove around his bramble-sprouting island
in an old Chevy with the top down,
watching the diaphanous stars

chariot race,
       brawled with God,
a heretical pilgrim
looking for a good enough dream
       or legacy, or team,
to forget and forgo
his rage
and be still enough to sleep
a turtle's hermetic sleep,
maybe inch
       his way toward the other side
         of what he already knew
wasn't Paradise, just
a quiet country road (certainly
       not the Long Island Expressway
on a Friday night during rush hour),
maybe
he would've liked
to hear R's version of "Round Midnight,"
       smoke an unfiltered Lucky Strike,
stretch his unambiguous legs,
    wonder
how things might've worked out
if he'd been born only half out of luck,
       only half
the wrong shade of blue,
maybe then
he could've educated himself enough
to understand
       why
he couldn't be a citizen of *any*thing,
stand straight up
       like a sycamore tree,
   be, you know, more
a part of things.

10

    My father's
immigrant eyes
flashed in the slats
of shivering rain
as he torched
a clothing warehouse
for insurance, while
I sat in the car, watching
his shadow sprinkle
a can of gasoline — poof
all six floors a blistering ladder of light
                    climbing
the sky, floating
           deep inside
the grid of my ten-year-old eyes,
the ash cloud falling
over the night — wondering

what if people are inside
what if the police come
what if mother finds out
why he wanted a witness

boomboomboom
rain hammering the hood
like fists

11

    I wake
out of a dream
of Abubunde's childhood face,
      his eyes still innocent,
tight balls of faith,

his flesh not yet peeled
apple rinds, oh
the unforgiven sins
	buried deep
in the soul's bottomless basement,
too far down to find
with a flashlight,
Monica
tucked deep
in sleep, her belly burgeoning
with our second son,
a smoky curl
	of thigh poking
out of a moment
so sweet
I watch the stars pass
deep above
this fertile island.

12

	Can
a man die
in a single English sentence?

December 15, 1972

Dear P,

. . . R killed himself two days ago . . . he was living in his car after he sold all his things to pay for two weeks of scream therapy after C left him and took her daughter . . . I saw him a week before he died . . . nothing left but pain . . . he wanted to talk to you but you were moving around . . . he couldn't reach you . . .
K

These words bounced
all the way from San Francisco

to Provincetown . . . but I
was "moving around" . . .
ignorant of the difference
I might have made.

13

     Our son,
Eli,
loves to grab hold
and fly across
the sacred lagoon
     of the living room
in a tango
of arms feet and screams,
     invents himself
one mistake at a time.
Born on the longest day of light,
his tiny fists clenched
as if against
all that was yet to come,
his black eyes excluding no one.
Now we high-step
around the house, two steps
forward, three back
and turn, do it over again,
     some nights,
when it's time to go to bed,
he points at the sky
and asks, But why?
The blackness
I think he means.
All the miles
of nothing.

14

    One day
when R was seven
his white mother
      took him aside
and said: Baby,
it hurts me to tell you
but your real daddy
was a black man.
You're only half white.
No, Daddy
isn't your father
and he doesn't
want you anymore.
Your brother and sister
can stay because
they're all white.
It's you or all of us.
It's not your fault
      but
your hair's getting curly
and your lips thick . . .
You got to go
live in a foster home.
I'm so sorry,
really
I am . . .

15

    Did Mr. Smith
suspect King Abubunde's mind
was about to go on a rampage?
That it was truth time?
    Did Mr. Smith

try to warn him not to listen
to the hundred black angels
singing in his ear?
    Some nights
R played something so fine
his quick scared eyes
became sphinxlike, dark
with a beveled-truth praise,
straight from the heart,
    and then
he'd rub his elegant hands
and laugh, Hey—
whaddya think of that, man?
    A blackbird
perched on his shoulder,
whispering
    maybe
he wasn't black *or* white
enough to survive,
    maybe
he was blurred,
like twilight.

16

    Marriage,
the daily rites
of who didn't cover
the leftovers, why the soap
isn't where it's supposed to be,
    the constant demand
of things wanting to be cooked,
cleaned, hugged and understood.
    Now
the trick is
not to think but drift

in ever-widening circles,
raking perfect camel humps
as the wind reshingles the lawn,
     and Monica
arranges lilacs, cuts, snaps
and places each flower
in window light.
     I barely recall
the man with my name
who played solitaire all night,
or what made him seem
like a stranger the morning
I left him behind
at a train station.
     Now
we have no one
but ourselves
to blame
for our happiness.

17

     "Up here
in Harlem," the president
of 125th Street Improvement District
tells the world
the next day,
     "things explode,
no one's innocent
for long."

18

     At night
Monica and I stand
in our backyard

watching Venus move
through the black sea
grass of space.
    Our house
was built in 1927
back when
this oblong island
was all farmland.
There's a photo
of the man who
made this house
with two enormous hands,
    standing
slumped
deep inside
    a smile
of pure
satisfaction.
    At night
the wind wraps
the cedars
    he planted
at the other end
of this century.

19

    Yesterday
everyone talked back,
never listened,
    now
Abubunde Mulocko
carries a revolver,
a bag of paint thinner,
is shouting, "It's on
    everybody

black gets out,"
    but before
anyone can
bullets split plaster,
everyone
    is glass
    is running
from his power
    toward
Judgment Day.

20

    Everyone's
got a position. Look
at the way R's white father
saw things:
    he weds a pregnant woman,
is married seven years when
she tells him R's the son
    of a black man
she met in a bar one night
while engaged to him.
    You got to
admit
that's a lot
for one Monday night
after the ball game.

    Maybe
the earth opened up
and swallowed him.

    Maybe
he was Satan.

21

My ring
slipped off my finger
        and I kept diving
for it
in the middle of a lake,
in the middle of a deepening
darkness—Monica yelling:
"It can be replaced,
                it's not us
you're diving after,
        please
come back,"
        but
I couldn't stop,
believing
        it was what
bound us,
glistening down there
under the uproar
where fish move in and out
of their shadows
in gleaming families,
        like a promise.

    We bought
our rings quickly,
just got off a subway
and bought them
wanting to be more
than ourselves,
our faces pressed
to the shiny glass
like children
        lost
in a grand speculation.

22

K sent me
the dream journal R kept:

*. . . on a train heading toward NYC where P has promised to meet me at Grand
Central Station under the clock, what I need he says is human beings bumping
against me I'm too self-absorbed (doesn't understand I never owned a self) but what
do I have to lose but my anonymity anyhow you can't argue with the pied piper of
guardian angels so I climb out of a smokecloud and look around at this huge domed
ceiling light pouring down with angels riding dust carpets and god in the stained
glass looking down at all his foolish folk hurrying everywhichway like slaves anxious
to be judged righteous despair leaking from their pantlegs boom boom boom of the
city outside I'm shaking head to toe sorry I ever left S F stop to watch a little black
boy tap-dancing to a boombox people clapping tossing coins in a hat his feet flying
fingers snapping eyes shut tight Mama Mama someone in the crowd is crying but no
one is listening I can see my face in the polished stones of his eyes feel myself all the
way back to my birth in an alley with old black women singing praise Mama Mama
how talented I am how much I have to live for, P tells me now it's raining everyone
running for cover the black boy still dancing like there aint no tomorrow . . .*

23

Everything
goes round
    and round
like the earth
    around the sun
or is it
    the other way around?
All
    R ever wanted
was a proud spine,
    aint like they
who got one
gonna miss a slice,
trick is

never ask
for love
    while you're
on your knees.

24

    Now all
anyone'll remember
    is flammable paint thinner
and the semiautomatic revolver
he brandished
like a scepter,
not his royal fire
his to and fro apostolic strut
and street-corner gospels,
not his soul stitched to his face in flames,
no, they'll remember
the sacrilege up his nose
all the minstrel halos
yanked out of scorched sleeves,
they'll remember Freddy's,
the stink of human torches
burning in a discounted Hades —
    not his shadow
reciting scripture with praise,
his mind stuffed with waves
of sloshing flammable hate juice,
    not that after twenty years
on 125th Street,
            his *street*,
his soul drowned in diluvium waters
    because it was winter
and God
soaked his furnace
and braided his telephone wires
into a crown of fire.

25

    My wife reads
the paper's obsequy aloud,
what took place at Freddy's Fashion Mart
      two days before Christmas:
where Kareem Brunner, 23, security guard,
his best job yet, he feels up to it,
tough but kindly mien,
he'll be a success one day,
was shot and burned dead,
along with—Olga Garcia, 19,
shopping for her father and brothers
who don't like her working so hard,
      but what the hell,
this is America, man,
pull your weight
or go down Moses—
      Angeline Marrero, 20,
daughter of a Pentecostal minister,
so sweet
he named her after an angel,
      listen
she didn't know how
to open a bank account,
      imagine that,
an angel with a bank account—
      Cynthia Martinez, 19,
anxious to turn 20, so eager
not to be an American teenager—
      Garnette Ramantar, 43,
the store manager,
      fresh from Guyana,
his wife so proud
he stays up late reading
at the kitchen table, what determination,
American know-how,

she rushes to see if his car
is parked outside Freddy's,
        it is,
Sweet Jesus, oh no
not Garnette — Luz Ramos, 20,
a salesclerk, two babies,
one three, the other nine months,
        this is her first job,
look it's like this, "You get a job,
it's bad; you don't, it's bad," her brother
José tells anyone
who'll listen, "it's all crap fuck*ing* politics" —
        the moment is a tree
of hallucinations — finally
Mayra Rentas, 22,
visiting her friend Luz,
worrying about last-minute shopping,
            nothing too expensive,
she's saving for college . . .

26

        Napoleon
the doorman
is interviewed on TV
on his way home from work,
stands on 125th Street
in front of a black hole
in the ground, shakes
his head, "Will this community
survive? Man, you
gotta be kidding."
Behind him, screams
(I imagine) ricochet
and tinsel angels
float
        in a whoosh of red air.

27

The last entry
in R's journal reads:

> . . . *P first brought me to these cliffs the most beautiful place in the world*
> *he said like the world was full of beauty I tried so hard to believe him I guess*
> *I'm going to ruin it for him I always envied the dead maybe it's like the ocean*
> *bottomless complete unto itself not needing anything from anyone unforgiving I*
> *wish I could forgive her the way her eyes got when she told me I had to go away*
> *she was five years younger than I am now when she had me once I saw her in a*
> *store and followed her as she shopped for kids' stuff touched all those pretty clothes*
> *smiling didn't she feed me her milk didn't I come out of her covered with her blood*
> *screaming holy jesus christ why wasn't there any love left . . .*

28

Often
Abubunde must've wondered
what went wrong and when—
was it on a Wednesday,
Monday or snowy Friday
when his soul started to die.

I wonder
what he did the night before
while Luz's radio sang
of innocent infatuation,
watch TV (he didn't own one),
read the Bible (he knew it by heart),
eat a last meal (no appetite),
think how his Mama,
a true believer,
made him promise
to make her proud?

29

    The ocean
lives exactly
one mile away,
churning like quicksilver,
all that matter
constantly swirling
down
      around
and under itself,
like shadows,
while our infant son
smiles
      at the night sky
as if he understands
why
in God's name
      so many
tiny lights
seem to shimmer
a moment longer,
      without mercy,
wonder,
      or forgiveness.

Living in the Past

2004

2

No one in this family ever suspects they're unhappy;
in fact, the less happy we are, the less we suspect it.
Uncle walks around with a straightedge razor tied round
his neck on a red string, screaming and pounding on things.
When he's angry, and he's always angry, he drops to a crouch
and screams until the veins in his neck bulge like steam pipes.
Mother locks herself, Grandma, and me in the toilet until he's flat.
We spend a lot of time in the toilet never suspecting anything.
Didn't everyone on Cuba Place have an uncle who hides
in a tiny room off the kitchen yelling at a police radio and writing
letters to dead presidents while reading girlie books all night?
Didn't everyone live in a house where everyone feels cheated,
ignored, and unredeemed?

3

Grandma climbs a chair to yell at God for killing
her only husband whose only crime was forgetting
where he put things. Finally, God misplaced him. Everyone
in this house is a razor, a police radio, a bulging vein.
It's too late for any of us, Grandma says to the ceiling.
She believes we are chosen to be disgraced and perplexed.
She squints at anyone who treats her like a customer, including
the toilet mirror, and twists her mouth into a deadly scheme.
Late at night I run at the mirror until I disappear. The day is over
before it begins, Grandma says, jerking the shade down over
its once rosy eye. She keeps her husband's teeth in a matchbox,
in perfumed paraffin; his silk skullcap (with its orthodox stains)
in the icebox, behind Uncle's Jell-O aquarium of floating lowlifes.
I know what Mrs. Einhorn said Mrs. Edels told Mr. Kook about us:
God save us from having one shirt, one eye, one child. I know
in order to survive. Grandma throws her shawl of exuberant birds
over her bony shoulders and ladles up yet another chicken thigh
out of the steaming broth of the infinite night sky.

4

Grandma peeps from behind her shades at everyone peeping at her.
The Italians are having people over in broad daylight, while the Slovaks
are grilling goats alive (this means a ten-year stink!), and the Ukrainians
are mingling on their porches, plotting our downfall. "Keep out of my yard,"
she cries in her sleep. Everyone sneaks around, has a hiding place.
Uncle's police radio calls all cars to a virgin abducted on Main Street,
while Mother binges on Almond Joys and Father sleepwalks through
the wilderness of the living room, Odysseus disguised as a Zionist,
or a pickled beet—"With my hands in my pockets and my pockets in my pants
watch the little girlies do the hootchie kootchie dance!" he sings every morning.
Nights, I sneak into the toilet, where Uncle jumps out of the tub, yelling "Boo!"
I hide behind my eyes where even I can't find me.

5

Old man Haas next door dresses in soiled sheets and sacrifices cats
in his backyard, whispering Grandma's maiden name. He wants us
gassed even if Hitler isn't going to invade Cuba Place. Nazis
are fortune-tellers and know everyone's secrets, Grandma thinks.
Bubbe, I say, either he's a Nazi or a Grand Wizard, he can't be both,
nobody's that evil! Good for him, she says, now he'll burn in hell
only five thousand years. He stands in the alley between our houses
snapping hedge shears, daring me to get past him, just once. One day
he steps on something Grandma drops in a dream and comes home
from the hospital with two empty pant legs and now Grandma
won't even look at the ceiling because what God gives with
the right hand he takes with the left.

6

Mother locks me and Grandma in the toilet until Uncle stops
pulverizing the door because one of the cashiers at the Paramount
looked at him funny and he pulled the curtain shut on Humphrey Bogart
and the bus driver didn't say hello again. I'm sick of hiding with Grandma
who spits on Mrs. Tillem's older sister Etta for giving her the evil eye
in the Quality Bakery in front of Mrs. Epstein who's there every time
something bad happens. Let something good happen and even Hitler
can't find her. I don't know about Mrs. Epstein, but I'm sick of waiting
like Grandma for the cherubim to deliver us out of Egypt just so
we can tell everyone to go to hell.

7

Grandma ties red strings to doorknobs, chairs, lamps, both her thumbs
because Mrs. Tillem complimented her hat, and now she has a nosebleed,
and old man Haas screams "Lousy Hebes" in his sleep as his swastika
lights blink in every window, and all four daughters (named Babe) goose-step
round the neighborhood, while Mr. Hildebrand's two three-legged reindeer
race up his roof toward statuesque bliss. Cossacks hung Grandma's cousin
Leopold's balls over the door like mistletoe. That's why she hates a season
that smells so good and never crosses her legs or eyes or shows anyone
her profile, why she opens her mouth only to scream, because dybbuks enter
us through the mouth, and she hates being a landlord even to the dead.

10

Almost every night Mr. Schwartzman wakes up Spinoza calm
in a pit named Auschwitz, opens his Lazarus eyes wide and looks
around at the dead eyeballs, broken fingers and mouths stuffed
with screams, his teeth tick, his kneecaps scrape, his nose big
as a blood sausage. For piano lessons I write his letters nobody answers,
about Mrs. Tillem's boardinghouse, where everybody stinks of herring
and moans in their sleep; about his job at the A&P providing for
everyone else's appetite. Not about what happened to his music or why
God spared him. Saturday mornings for two years he speaks Yiddish
as I write my twelve-year-old English until the day I find him hanging
in his closet with a note pinned to his tie: "One does not perish among Jews."

11

Everyone dickers with God. Everyone gets something.
Grandma gets one dead husband who does nothing
but read Torah and complain, the kitchen ceiling where
all her curses live rent free, a lifetime of oy veis . . . Uncle gets
his wieners, eight varieties of sauerkraut, five newspapers spread
over the kitchen table like a vast strategy, the Paramount screen
where he pulls curtains shut on Marlene D who shaves her legs
four times a day. Father gets free room and board, a coal burner
to intimidate, all the blame. Mother gets the lower left half of
the icebox, where she hides bacon, Popsicles, all her glee.
I get the best hiding places, Uncle's girlie books, the stained glass
attic window where the wind sings of inner and outer things,
as Martin Buber said, what are they but things — "O secrecy
without a secret! O accumulation of information!" I get faith
and intuition and 5763 years of longing and despair, a passion
for hearsay, boogying and epistemology . . .

12

Before Uncle burned Grandma's house down
he burned down the Dubinsky brothers' junkyard barn
because he used to climb our roof to watch their sister
dance naked in her bedroom. Grandma says only a Russian slut
doesn't know to pull a shade over her big teats when she dances
for the devil. Everybody on Cuba Place watches her but they
only knock Uncle's teeth out. She blames God for putting
a junkyard behind our house. Uncle blames only the barn.
When he burns her house down in the middle of the night
she says only one word, she says, "See!"

13

Mr. Schwartzman survived the Nazis but not Cuba Place, where
he takes long Saturday walks with his five dead children
who ride a carousel round the inside of his cracked eyeballs,
each a continent, a résumé filed at Auschwitz, where Gertrud Kolmar,
his older sister's best friend, also was murdered, her poems
scratched in blood, flying over the Urals, singing, "Out of darkness
I come, a woman, I carry a child, and have forgotten whose it is."
He reads her at the back of his candlelit eyes, his kaddish voice
wears a tallis and skullcap, praising her soul's dark soliloquy: "I am
a continent that will sink without a sound into the sea."

14

The Cinemascope is too big for the screen so Alan Ladd
rides off into the curtains and the gangsters in the B-picture
look like the men in the pool hall where Father owns
peanut machines. The lights come on and we shake Father
and follow everyone out to walk home under the elms and
sycamores, through the crickets, fireflies and honeysuckle,
Mother's hand in mine and Father a step ahead, bent under
the streetlights whose shadows curl his fedora into a snake
and squeeze his face into a fist. Friday nights in spring nobody
talks about lugging syrup cases up factory stairs or stopping
to breathe in icy alleyways or counting greasy coins until
your thumbs blister or all the bills we can't pay . . . In spring
we walk under the Rochester stars, chilled and stuck-up,
Father says, his lips silently answering old insults, Mother's
blue eyes black with a sadness she can't say, all the way
to our house on Cuba Place, where the porch light sways
in the breeze off Lake Ontario and the fence needs painting
and the kitchen sags under our weight, where Mother and I
were born and I am the best thing that ever happened to her,
she whispers, putting me to bed, back when the world was new
and Alan Ladd was already too big for the neighborhood.

15

On Saturdays I follow Father through factories, pool halls,
tool & die shops, lathes echoing off cinderblock as we lug
dollies piled high with syrup, ice cream in hissing dry ice,
under blue fluorescent clouds in meat freezers, slipping in
greasy sawdust, his thumbless left hand zipping razor-edged
metal coffins, *zziiiinngggoooopppp!*, tossing in candy, cigarettes,
Mother's tuna salad, unclogging hot and cold colored snakes
inside soda and coffee machines, cursing and praying to screws
nuts and wires he means nothing to, kibbitzing over his always
moving shoulder to men in overalls and suits at DuPonts, Gerbers,
Bonds, Bausch and Lomb's (everyone a war hero!), handing out
free coffee, cashews, Mounds bars, women giggling as his big smile
swaggers down hallways . . . until we get home in the dark, stinking
of chocolate, coffee grounds, powdered sugar, soured mayonnaise,
his hands red and swollen from slapping a million backs.

16

On Wednesday mornings Grandma packs shopping bags
with potato salad, sour pickles, bundles of girlie books,
as Uncle yells, "All salami, no bologna for Izzy, Ma!"
tugging at his shoelaces under a signed photo of Mae West—
everything in his room hangs from the ceiling, police radio,
butcher knife, fountain pens, a rhyming dictionary. "It's time
SOMEBODY went to see him! Everybody acts like he's dead
but *who's* eating all this goddamn salami!" Only Grandma says
anything: "God suck the eyes out of my head and put boils
on my tongue! He who lives with a devil becomes one!"
We all know who SOMEBODY is—he wants *me* to visit
my crazy uncle Izzy at the State Hospital! Izzy, who bit
a Ukrainian woman in Levi's grocery for bending over
to taste a pickle, whom Uncle pushed off the roof for watching
the Dubinsky girl dance naked in her bedroom, which everyone
knew was his privilege, whom Grandma says kaddish for!
"Don't take it personally," Mr. Schwartzman says, rocking
on his porch with all the other DPs, "everyone needs a witness."
Nothing is personal in the middle of the 20th Century, he says,
each of us a spoonful of worm stew. In another 248 days
I'll be bar mitzvahed and leave this valley of endless weeping.

18

Being chosen doesn't mean what Grandma thinks,
Mr. Schwartzman says. It's not a boast but an obligation,
as Abraham said, a chosenness to sanctify the name of God.
"Of all the families on earth . . . will I visit upon you all your
iniquities." We are a choosing people, the dawn and the dusk,
the challenge and the test. Yes, but after everything that happened
to him, did *he* believe in God? I ask. He shuts his eyes and says:
"Spinoza believed he who revenges lives in misery and enemies
of faith are its greatest defenders, that passion without reason
is blind as reason with passion is death, that nothing we do
affects our fate and nothing is our fate. Martin Buber said,
'God's existence cannot be proved. Yet he who dares to speak
of it, bears witness . . .' The year Columbus discovered America,
Ferdinand discovered the Jews. Thus: the Inquisition without
which there'd be no Spinoza, or a boychick on Cuba Place.
You ask what I believe? I believe in Darwin and Beethoven.
In Gertrud Kolmar's longing for ecstasy and heritage, and
most of all, I believe in believing, and in Talmud there is faith
and knowledge, so according to this Gospel, I believe in God."

20

Every night at Kodak as he sweeps the floors,
Father dreams of the vending machines he'll buy.
He comes home after dawn and sits at the kitchen table
staring out the window, his lips silently moving.
He wants the biggest vending business in upstate
New York, that's why he buys new machines
without paying for the old ones, Mother says,
so he can be a big shot. All the things she never says
give her headaches so I rub her neck as she holds ice
to her eyes. After someone on the phone yells, she
eats ice cream and Mars bars. "What must you think
of me, crying all day? Please don't be like me, don't
agree with everyone . . ." Father falls asleep pulling
his pants off but soon there's coffee in J. C. Penney's
and five kinds of soda in Abe's Pool Hall . . . while
Uncle pays all the bills, walks around in torn boxers
making us watch TV and eat in the dark. When he
tells me to draw a "pic'chur of a horse drawin' a wagon,"
I draw a horse with a pencil in its hoof and hide as he
rips it up, raves all night. In this house, where everyone's
a genius, talks only to themselves, and spits three times
over their left shoulder, everything is a riddle.

21

Mr. Schwartzman writes fifteen letters to a dead older brother,
Reuben, who, like Spinoza, grinds eyeglasses for a living.
"God only knows why he lives in Berlin. It's a beautiful city,
long clean avenues . . . but they murdered him!" Five letters to
a dead daughter, Rebecca, who lives in Paris which is beautiful
at night, like glass, like Mozart . . . He unbuttons his vest and sighs—
"Four children and her singing career flourishes! Sons are wonderful
but a daughter looks after you . . . Gertrud died childless: 'Oh the stillness . . .
in my womb: the axe . . . my child.'" He keeps his letters in a shoebox
in the closet next to the bed that lives in the wall like a ghost.

23

Every Saturday Mr. Schwartzman lets me sneak him
into the Paramount by knocking three times until Uncle
opens the back door. According to the movies everyone
in America is a gangster or a hero, he says. He likes
Gary Cooper because he saves everyone. God is the hero
of the Bible, but he saved almost no one. In Europe it's more
like the Bible, where everyone is asked to sacrifice something.
For what? Yetzer Ha-ra, the evil desire inherent in everyone,
lived in Abraham and also in Mr. Schwartzman, who sacrificed
a wife, all three sons and two daughters. A hero is what everyone
wanted but Gary Cooper must have been busy saving someone else.

24

We walk through the lilac stink to the front doors and
down a long hallway to the elevators which Uncle bangs
open, then down a corridor to a screened locked door
where a black man says, "Lo, Moe, you're late this week."
Uncle gives him a bundle of girlie books and leads us across
a cafeteria to a table where a small pink man licks his lips.
"Izzy, this is your nephew," Uncle says. Izzy smiles, kicking
his feet. Bald and rosy, with Mother's blue eyes and Grandma's
turnip nose, he stuffs his cheeks with everything Moe unpacks:
celery bologna pickles sardines coleslaw . . . until the black man
sticks a spoon down his throat making him gurgle and pump
out a hissing spray into a pail, a spool swinging on his chin . . .
"Atta boy," Uncle says, uncapping a pen, "now write your name!"
Izzy writes in block letters, his face red and swollen and then
the black man takes his bundle and Izzy's hand and they go
back across the cafeteria down the long echoing linoleum.

27

Spuming a perish melody, Mr. Schwartzman rocks on his porch,
remembering how they lined up in cornstalk rows, his wife Dore
and sons Michael and Jacob and Nahum and daughters Rebecca
and Leah, naked on the lip of the ravine . . . one falling atop another
like stones into a black pool . . . He recalls this because it's Shabbos
and the DPs are marching to shul like dead weights on one of God's
scales, measuring heaven, hell and everything trapped between.
He combs his bald spot left to right, picks at his liver spots, his mind
an original garden without finials whose curious leaves mirror the
genius of the universe . . . he stood there watching a monarch butterfly
in the bright spring air, its wings inviting a miracle of divine intervention . . .

32

The Dubinsky brothers dance the kazatsky atop a mountain
of old sinks and glittering glass, their arms folded like crucifixes,
chests heaving like cannons. Father says only the Russians think
dancing is kicking and spitting vodka while breaking dishes on
your head, only the Russians prefer tables to floors for dancing
and lovemaking. Only the Russians get stuck with their arms
crossed and right leg stuck out until Monday morning when
it's not showing off but showing up, bright and early, to get kicked
all the way back to Saturday night, which stands waving a red lamp
at the end of eternity like a Cossack singing, Dance dance dance
for all you're worth, which is nothing, not a goddamn thing!

33

My bar mitzvah is going to be in The Grand Ballroom
of the Sheraton Hotel. Mother says: We live behind a junkyard
and can't afford cement in our basement but he's throwing
the biggest party since Moses heard voices. This is *our* opportunity
to show everyone we're alive and kicking, Father yells, anyone
can rent a backroom. But why pay ten years for one night,
she yells back. To have a night to remember, he says, she thinks
too small, debt is how you establish credit, the more the better,
that's why he keeps buying new machines, doesn't own insurance
or belong to a temple — he wants to owe everyone, even God.
All I want is a bowling party, for it all to be over with . . . at night
Mother eats tuna fish out of a can, with a spoon, sighing . . .

35

One Saturday morning I find Mr. Schwartzman turning
on a piano string in his closet, his eyes drained of experience,
while I, and what's left of my childhood, get stuck in one place.
The world, he quoted Buber, permits itself to be experienced,
but has no concern in the matter. I'm as tall as he is, though
his feet don't touch the ground. Even now I don't understand
why he put his suit and tie on but not his shoes or socks.

36

When I start bawling, Mr. Leonard, my seventh-grade teacher,
keeps me after school. We were reading how every species
overproduces because only the strong adapt and I wondered
if Mr. Schwartzman was too weak. "Every memory leaves
a bruise, a terrible doubt," he said when I asked why he stared
at the ground when he walked. "Cioran, a crazy Carpathian,
said consciousness is a disease and Gertrud's mind attacked her
like a hyena. Thinking is what's unforgivable, be afraid of yourself . . .
I stare because I can't stop looking for scraps of food . . ."

37

Singing Al Jolson, Father shaves with a great splashing,
eyes blinking, fat bottom lip thrust out, hiking his pants
as he tells the mirror all the great things he'll do that day . . .
Chasing or chased, he doesn't stand still long enough
to hear what he's thinking, Grandma says. Five foot one
and bald as the chickens she boils Fridays, nose pitted,
barrel chest worn high over his buckle, fear is the secret
to success, he says, naming all the big shots afraid of him.
He makes this look, cocks his eyes, "Be interested only in
what *you're* saying." He asks me how I feel about what he
thinks, then comes over and turns around to answer himself.
He stuck his thumb in a button machine, didn't even blink
as the blade sliced, then bought an old Ford with the insurance
and painted it yellow and called it The First Yellow Cab Co. of America
after The First Church of Christ in the middle of Main Street.

38

Three times a week Rabbi Runes comes to tutor me
and cough up phlegm in the sink Grandma scours
the minute he leaves. He stinks of tobacco, his teeth,
fingers, beard stained yellow. He screams if I look at
his hairy moles until Mother says I'm sensitive and
high-strung (my muscles tied too high and tight?) and
he nods, Shore shore, and sucks a Parliament to ash.
My birthday is in one month so he threatens to hang me
next to his photo of Rebbe Friedlander, head of the Big Shul,
who's as good as I'm evil. Every time Grandma opens a door
he breaks wind to show her what a piece of dreck she is.
When he leaves she screams, "God sends him to spit on
my dishes and still he's not happy, he has to leave a stink
that chokes even the dead . . ."

44

My first morning as a man I practice with a razor,
like learning the piano, Mother says, it needs practice.
"Bubbe, did you brush your tooth this morning?" I ask,
everything's too quiet—*krrraccckkkkkk* goes her rocker—
"Even dogs won't piss on your grave!" she yells. Mother
comes in the kitchen wearing her new emerald gown
and best fake pearls, her hair stiff and shiny, eyes and
cheeks so polished and dusted I forget to be scared . . .
"Well, bar mitzvah boy, how do I look, okay?" Great,
I say, putting on my suit and boiled-white shirt and blue
silk tie and black buckle shoes that snap like crickets.
Father comes out in pinstripes and a red polka-dot tie,
his big bottom lip thrust out. "Help him knot his tie," says
Mother, so he yanks at me, yells to stop moving, stands
back to look in the mirror, where, his hand on my shoulder,
he smiles at himself . . .

50

He didn't hate himself, Mr. Schwartzman said,
he was just tired of the arguments in his head.
"Jews argue to change only their own mind
and everyone on Cuba Place is forgotten, left behind,
except you, my boy. You have time." He said this,
his musical hands on my shoulders, two days before
I find him hanging. These words, my bar mitzvah gift.

51

Mother smiles from the colored lights as
words scrape up my throat and come out
my mouth—I'm singing the blessing before
the reading of the Law—"Borchu es adonoi
hamvoroch . . . Boruch adonoi hamvoroch l'olom . . .
Boruch atto adonoi, elohainu melech ho'olom,
asher bochar bonu mikol hoamim . . . adonoi . . ."
the rabbi singing too, then the congregation—
"This is the Torah which Moses placed before
the children of Israel . . . a tree of life to those
who take hold of it . . . its ways are pleasant and
all its paths are peace . . ." the words singing inside
and outside my body—"Blessed art Thou, O Lord
our God, King of the universe . . . Creator of all
the worlds, who sayeth and performest, who
speakest and fulfillest, for all thy words are true
and just . . ."—tears in my mouth, hot and sweet—
"Have compassion . . . for it is the source of our life . . .
Blessed art Thou, O Lord, who makest Zion rejoice
in her children . . ."—singing to Mother whose hair
is yellow fire—"Gladden us, Lord our God . . . bring joy
to our hearts . . . that his light should never go out . . ."

53

"Rest now and let your father say his blessing—you
sang like an angel, an angel," Rabbi Friedlander says
as Father moves up to the Book and takes a big breath
and cries out, "Blessed is the One Who has freed me
from the punishment due this boy . . ." and steps aside
as the rabbi moves forward and back and I lift off
the floor into the air and rise toward Mother, high
above the rabbi and Father, until I'm swaying in and
out of the glass light, turning above the bobbing heads
and exploding hands as the men sing ". . . *mazal tov
und simmun tov, simmun tov und mazal tov* . . ." their feet
and hands jumping as Father and his brothers dance,
singing ". . . *simchah simchah* . . ." the words lifting
around me as I float out of my body into the glassy fire . . .
and beyond . . . into the eyes of God . . .

54

A boy has one bar mitzvah but becomes a man
many times, Mr. Schwartzman said when I wondered
if I'd be any good at being one. It wasn't the biggest
bar mitzvah, but big enough. Father argued all night
with his brothers, even while waltzing Mother,
her eyes shut, as if afraid to see her happiness.
I danced Grandma around a cake shaped like the Empire
State Building and a chopped liver Eiffel Tower. "Smile
for posterity," the photographer said, as Father and I
clinked glasses in our Fashion Park suits, rooster-
crested shirts, white carnations in our lapels, "and look
thankful" . . . the way Father looked bursting into my room
each morning full of pep and high hopes, yelling, "Up and at
'em, we gotta get a jump on 'em, kiddo!" . . . yes, us against
the world . . . all of us, the living and the dead, wandering
in an endless epiphany in which only our grief belongs to us,
and what remains of our desire to colonize heaven.

64

The glass in our attic window wasn't real stained glass
but colored bottle glass, the kind you saw in all
the old houses on Cuba Place. Displaced glass used by
displaced people to effect an aura of good fortune
and civility. That's why we watered, hoed, and surveyed
our gardens with such devotion, pleading with God
to do right by every peony, cucumber and turnip, why
every Saturday men shined old Chevys and Plymouths
with beeswax and vinegar, and every spring women sang
in ten languages while hanging wash and picking cherries,
blackberries and peaches, and all of Rochester was one vast
walloping stink of lilac covering every walk, porch and fancy
with a pungent cloud of purple and white petals, why
American flags waved in every yard and men in overalls
and shirtsleeves whistled the national anthem, straining
to hear the Yankee game buried deep in static, why so much
was expected from a place where everyone was more than
themselves, where, no matter how far down you started from,
you began again from the beginning, with the same Godful longing . . .

65

After Mother died we drove around Cuba Place,
up Rauber and down Hixon to Thomas, and around
Widman to the liquor store where the Big Shul used to be.
The cake shaped like the Empire State Building, that Father
insisted on, is the only thing about my bar mitzvah that
interests Eli. "Where's everyone in the stories you tell me
at bedtime?" he asks when we stop in front of my house.
"Living in the past," I say. Yes, even Billy Sanders, who wore
his hair in a DA and died in Vietnam. "No," says my wife,
"they're all dead," meaning: it's time to say good-bye.
The windows are boarded up, the Dubinsky brothers'
junkyard is an empty lot, and the big oak that stood
outside my bedroom window is a hole in the ground.

66

We need a new car, my wife reminds me. I sit at my desk,
open books, scratch my head. One needs to be practical,
take money from here, put it there. Everyone knows how
to do this. But I can't. I hate all those numbers marching
around like high-school bands. I hate being precise. Also,
I love my old car, it's so loyal, patient, manufactured.
It drove us to Maine on our honeymoon and through
a blizzard when my wife was in labor. It's not a living thing,
it has an engine, not a brain, a transmission, not a soul.
It doesn't remember singing the Stones' "Satisfaction"
the night Mother died, watching the ocean swallow
everything. It knows it's time to leave, that it's falling
apart, rusting. But I can't bear starting over again.
At night I go outside and reminisce, like an idiot.

67

Mother's Yahrzeit is on the sixth day of Av 5758.
Praise the living light and sing the name,
her secret private name, in no one's ear but mine.
Praise the evening of the day before the endless night.
Leave nothing behind, forget no article of clothes or candlestick.
Praise the night, which gives nothing back,
not even her name which will not pass this way again

Lord.

68

It was only possible to live in the past, where life is organized,
Martin Buber said. But all those stories swallowed by the earth,
all those dreams rotting in unmarked graves, all those souls
defeated by the rain . . . "Yes," Mr. Schwartzman sighed,
"they live in the past, like stowaways."

69

This morning I'm tired of the same newspapers, and arguments.
I'm tired of sticking the same legs into the same pants,
the same hands poking out of the same sleeves, going west
and then east, heating up the same tea, watching the same sun
rise over the same horizon, the same trees shedding the same leaves.
Tired of climbing the same stairs to look out the same window
at the same street, tired of shaking the same hands, opening and
closing the same doors, dreaming the same dreams, saying hello
good morning happy birthday I'm so sorry please forgive me.

70

At camp in the Connecticut woods my wife slow-danced
to "The Long and Winding Road" in a polka-dot dress,
the cool lake air breeze on her cheeks as Richie's breath
gurgled in her ear, his sweaty hand snaking along her waist,
egging her north then south on the splintered deck . . . I shift
the baby's weight, listening with our five-year-old son as
she explains how she bowed to fit her head to his shoulder,
her eyes closed, the same gray eyes that close for me, closing for
that twelve-year-old moron, her legs swaying as they do now,
the same blossoming in her cheeks, the glow of her raisin hair
as he kissed her, her first, there, under the canopy of floating stars,
the music and lake stars swooning, all of it now forever lost
deep in the scented woods of a Connecticut evening.

71

Late at night, in bed, my wife remembers Juan
who told his dying father he was dying too, and
had joined the Catholic Church so they could be
friends in heaven. She loved his stories about his
father's chocolate factory, how all Spain stunk of it,
the bullfighters he painted and loved not so secretly . . .
She says her name the way he did, softly, on the tip
of her tongue, as if tasting her soul . . . I understand,
ten years is a long time to love someone, and be
young together. After he died all his friends came
to see the film he made about the waiting room
of an AIDS clinic, *One Foot on a Banana Peel,*
the Other in a Grave. She'd tell him everything
and he'd sit there, at his drafting board, listening
to her every word, as if it were precious.

73

"In the camp," Mr. Schwartzman said, "infinity was a comfort.
Now it's an assembly line, soup cans buttons shoes faces on TV . . .
like the lines of men women and children marching into the woods
to the ravine when the crematorium broke down, all their stories
of regret and triumph, their pleas to remain human a moment longer . . .
an infinity without heaven or hell, just endless blackness, beyond
which there's nothing, not even an idea to wonder or worry about . . ."

"All real living is meeting . . ." Martin Buber said, "true beings
are lived in the present, the life of objects is in the past."
It was Mr. Schwartzman's ambition to live in Buber's mind
like a grand hotel high in the Swiss Alps, not exactly heaven
or God, but far enough away from where we live our real lives.

It's Sunday Morning in Early November

and there are a lot of leaves already.
I could rake and get a head start.
The boys' summer toys need to be put
in the basement. I could clean it out
or fix the broken storm window.
When Eli gets home from Sunday school,
I could take him fishing. I don't fish
but I could learn to. I could show him
how much fun it is. We don't do as much
as we used to do. And my wife, there's
so much I haven't told her lately,
about how quickly my soul is aging,
how it feels like a basement I keep filling
with everything I'm tired of surviving.
I could take a walk with my wife and try
to explain the ghosts I can't stop speaking to.
Or I could read all those books piling up
about the beginning of the end of understanding . . .
Meanwhile, it's such a beautiful morning,
the changing colors, the hypnotic light.
I could sit by the window watching the leaves,
which seem to know exactly how to fall
from one moment to the next. Or I could lose
everything and have to begin over again.

Talking to Ourselves

A woman in my doctor's office last week
couldn't stop talking about Niagara Falls,
the difference between dog and deer ticks,
how her oldest boy, killed in Iraq, would lie
with her at night in the summer grass, singing
Puccini. Her eyes looked at me but saw only
the saffron swirls of the quivering heavens.

Yesterday, Mr. Miller, our tidy neighbor,
stopped under our lopsided maple to explain
how his wife of sixty years died last month
of Alzheimer's. I stood there, listening to
his longing reach across the darkness with
each bruised breath of his eloquent singing.

This morning my five-year-old asked himself
why he'd come into the kitchen. I understood
he was thinking out loud, personifying himself,
but the intimacy of his small voice was surprising.

When my father's vending business was failing,
he'd talk to himself while driving, his lips
silently moving, his black eyes deliquescent.
He didn't care that I was there, listening,
what he was saying was too important.

"Too important," I hear myself saying
in the kitchen, putting the dishes away,
and my wife looks up from her reading
and asks, "What's that you said?"

Specimen

I turned sixty in Paris last year.
We stayed at the Lutetia,
where the Gestapo headquartered
during the war, my wife, two boys, and me,
and several old Vietnamese ladies
carrying poodles with diamond collars.

Once my father caught a man
stealing cigarettes out of one
of his vending machines.
He didn't stop choking him
until the pool hall stunk of excrement
and the body dropped to the floor
like a judgment.

When I was last in Paris
I was dirt poor, hiding
from the Vietnam War.
One night, in an old church,
I considered taking my life.
I didn't know how to be so young
and not belong anywhere, stuck
among so many perplexing melodies.

I loved the low white buildings,
the ingratiating colors, the ancient light.
We couldn't afford such luxury.
It was a matter of pride.
My father died bankrupt one week
before his sixtieth birthday.
I didn't expect to have a family;
I didn't expect happiness.

At the Lutetia everyone
dressed themselves like specimens
they'd loved all their lives.
Everyone floated down
red velvet hallways
like scintillating music
you hear only once or twice.

Driving home, my father said,
"Let anyone steal from you
and you're not fit to live."
I sat there, sliced by traffic lights,
not belonging to what he said.
I belonged to a scintillating
and perplexing music
I didn't expect to hear.

The Summer People

Santos, a strong, friendly man,
who built my wife's sculpture studio,
fixed everything I couldn't,
looked angry in town last week.
Then he stopped coming. We wondered
if we paid him enough, if he envied us.
Once he came over late to help me catch a bat
with a newspaper and trash basket.
He liked that I laughed at how scared I got.

We're "year rounds," what the locals call
summer people who live here full time.
Always in a hurry, the summer people honk a lot,
own bigger cars and houses. Once I beat a guy
in a pickup to a parking space, our summer sport.
"Lousy New Yorker!" he cried.

Every day now men from Guatemala, Ecuador,
and Mexico line up at the railroad station.
They know that they're despised,
that no one likes having to share their rewards,
or being made to feel spiteful.

When my uncle Joe showed me the shotgun
he kept near the cash register
to scare the black migrants
who bought his overpriced beer and cold cuts
in his grocery outside of Rochester, N.Y.,
his eyes blazed like emerald suns.
It's impossible to forget his eyes.

At parties the summer people
who moved here after 9/11
talk about all the things they had to give up.
It's beautiful here, they say, but everything
is tentative and strange,
as if the beauty isn't theirs to enjoy.

When I'm tired, my father's accent
scrapes my tongue like a scythe.
He never cut our grass or knew
what grade I was in. He worked days,
nights, and weekends, but failed anyway.
Late at night, when he was too tired to sleep,
he'd stare out the window so powerfully
the world inside and outside
our house would disappear.

In Guatemala, after working all day,
Santos studied to be an architect.
He suffered big dreams, his wife said.
My wife's studio is magnificent.
We'd hear him up there in the dark,
hammering and singing, as if
he were the happiest man alive.

The Magic Kingdom

It's a beautiful January Sunday morning,
the first morning of the new year,
and my old dogs limp behind me up the beach
as my sons scour the ocher sand like archivists
seeking the day's quota of mystery.
To them it's all a magical kingdom,
their minds tiny oceans of good and evil strategies,
the hard traffic of dreams
enclosed by a flourishing expectation.

We came here for the ripening light,
the silence of the enormous sky; to exult
in the shy jewels of sea glass
polished by the tides of the wind,
in the forlorn shrieks and chortling cries of gulls
rising and falling between their world and ours.
To be where it was lush,
lonely and secret enough.

At the edge of things,
in the shimmering spray
and flawless sparkle of seashells,
under the lonely momentum of clouds
lugging their mysterious cargoes all the way
to the horizon and back,
each a wish, a gift
that must be returned.

I never thought I'd have so much to give up;
that the view from this side of my life
would be so precious. Bless
these filaments of sea grass,

this chorus of piping plovers
and bickering wrens, each mile
these arthritic animals tag behind,
sniffing tire ruts, frothy craters of rotting driftwood,
lacy seaweed and scuttling crabs,
after something deliciously foul . . .

Bless the plenitude of the suffering mind . . .
its endless parade of disgrace
and spider's web of fear, the hunger
of the soul that expects to be despised
and cast out, the unforgiving ghosts
I visit late at night when only God is awake . . .

Bless this ice-glazed garden of bleached stones
strewn like tiny pieces of moonlight
in sand puddles,
the wind's grievous sigh,
the singing light,
the salt, the salt!

Most of all bless these boys
shivering in the chill light,
their fragile smallness and strange intransigence,
so curious and shining. Bless
their believing happiness will make them happy;
that the ocean is magical, a kingdom
where we go to be human,
and grateful.

Grief

My wife is happier this morning.
Valentine's Day, the kids and I went all out,
candy, cards, heart-shaped cookies.
Gus, our smooth Fox Terrier,
mopes around, tail down, grieving
for our black Lab mix, Benya,
who still sleeps in our boys' room.
Gary, my wife's younger brother,
no longer lives in his photos on her dresser.
He prefers to stand behind our maple,
hands in pockets, trying not to interfere.
My friend Yehuda still drops by without calling.
Right now, he's marching backwards
around my study, making the sound
of every instrument in the Israeli Philharmonic,
hoping to cheer me up. I used to think
the dead preferred their own company.
They don't. They prefer ours.

The Garden

In memory of Joel Dean

Years before I moved next door,
Joel gave Jack gardening books
and Jack made a garden out of
his passion for geometry, and chance.
He raked, clawed, and watered each
peculiar vision until the daylilies
were good company and the azaleas
were immaculate and dignified.

I used to stand on my side of the red cedars,
listening to Jack's endless scraping,
envying his devotion. I was alone then
but understood love was a gift,
a vast, unbroken conversation.

Yesterday, Jack scraped all morning,
on his hands and knees, weeding,
plucking musical vines. Ask and he'll say
their forty-six years was a garden of exquisite design.

It's best to remember the peonies,
the quaint delirium of lilacs, and Joel
at the back door enjoying the reunion
of cardinals, robins, and pesky blue jays
speaking the language of color and delight,
the language of chance and endless change.

Why

is this man sitting here weeping
in this swanky restaurant
on his sixty-first birthday, because
his fear grows stronger each year,
because he's still the boy running
all out to first base, believing
getting there means everything,
because of the spiders climbing
the sycamore outside his house
this morning, the elegance of
a civilization free of delusion,
because of the boyish faces
of the five dead soldiers on TV,
the stoic curiosity in their eyes,
their belief in the righteousness
of sacrifice, because innocence
is the darkest place in the universe,
because of the Iraqis on their hands
and knees, looking for a bloody button,
a bitten fingernail, evidence of
their stolen significance, because
of the primitive architecture
of his dreams, the brutal egoism
of his ignorance, because he believes
in deliverance, the purity of sorrow,
the sanctity of truth, because of
the original human faces of his wife
and two boys smiling at him across
this glittering table, because of
their passion for commemoration,
their certainty that goodness continues,
because of the spiders clinging to
the elegance of each moment, because
getting there still means everything?

My Wife

My wife's younger brother took heroin and died
in the bed he slept in as a boy across
the hall from the one she slept in as a girl.

He sold the pot he grew in their basement.
She'd leave work to take him to the clinic
but she understood she had to save herself.

No one saves themselves. Before I met my wife
I'd put on anything clean. My life dragged behind,
like a heavy shadow. I was resigned to anonymity.
I wanted to sleep. She gave my pain a bride.

Two months after he died, we hold hands
across a black sea, trying not to despise
the drunk at the next table, who doesn't
even try not to listen. It's best not to think
about the pain. To shut your eyes and float.

Our kids were jumping on our bed, windmilling,
in love with their capacity for delight.
When she answered the phone she shut her eyes.

He was a sweet young man who looked,
when we took him on his thirtieth birthday
to a restaurant filled with beautiful women,
as if he wanted to live forever.

When we visited his grave, the kids and I
wandered around in a city of the dead
and I could see her down the long avenues,
pulling weeds and staring at the ground.

At night she walks in the dark downstairs.
I know what she wants, to go to him the way
she goes to our boys when they're frightened,
to place herself between him and the pain.

What I Like and Don't Like

I like to say hello and good-bye.
I like to hug but not shake hands.
I prefer to wave or nod. I enjoy
the company of strangers pushed
together in elevators or subways.
I like talking to cab drivers
but not receptionists. I like
not knowing what to say.
I like talking to people I know
but care nothing about. I like
inviting anyone anywhere.
I like hearing my opinions
tumble out of my mouth
like toddlers tied together
while crossing the street,
trusting they won't be squashed
by fate. I like greeting-card clichés
but not dressing up or down.
I like being appropriate
but not all the time.
I could continue with more examples
but I'd rather give too few
than too many. The thought
of no one listening anymore —
I like that least of all.

Blunt

I hate the idea of being asked
to bow down before
something in whose name
millions have been sacrificed.
I want nothing to do
with a soul. I hate
its crenulated edges
and bottomless pockets,
its guileless, eyeless stare.
I hate the idea of paradise,
where the souls of Socrates
and Machiavelli are made
to live side by side. If
I have to believe in something,
I believe in despair. In its
antique teeth and sour breath
and long memory. To it
I bequeath the masterpiece
of my conscience, the most
useless government of all.
The truth gets the table scraps
of my dignity. It can do
what it likes with the madman
of my desire and the conjurer
of my impotence. I prefer
to see myself as an anomaly
involuntarily joined to
an already obsolete
and transitory consciousness
that must constantly save
itself from itself,

as a peculiar instinct
for happiness that
sustained me for a brief
but interesting time.

The Adventures of 78 Charles Street

For thirty-two years Patricia Parmelee's yellow light
has burned all night
in her kitchen down the hall in 2E.
Patricia—I love to say her name—Par-me-lee!
knows where, across the street,
Hart Crane wrote "The Bridge,"
the attic Saul Bellow holed up in
furiously scribbling *The Adventures of Augie March*,
the rooftop Bing Crosby yodeled off,
dreaming of Broadway, the knotty,
epicene secrets of each born-again townhouse.
Indeed, we, Patricia and me, reminisce
about tiny Lizzie and Joe Pasquinnucci,
one deaf, the other near-blind,
waddling hand-in-hand down the hall,
up the stairs, in and out of doors,
remembering sweetening Sicilian peaches,
ever-blooming daylilies, a combined one hundred
and seventy years of fuming sentence fragments,
elastic stockings, living and outliving
everyone on the south side of Charles Street.

How Millie Kelterborn, a powerhouse
of contemptuous capillaries inflamed
with memories of rude awakenings,
wrapped herself in black chiffon
when her knocked-up daughter Kate married a Mafia son
and screamed "Nixon, blow me!"
out her fifth-floor window,
then dropped dead face-first
into her gin-spiked oatmeal.
How overnight Sharon in 4E

became a bell-ringing Buddhist
explaining cat litter, America, pleurisy, multiple orgasms,
why I couldn't love anyone who loved me.

And Archie McGee in 5W, one silver-cross earring,
a tidal wave of dyed black hair,
jingling motorcycle boots, Jesus boogying
on each enraged oiled biceps, screaming
four flights down at me for asking
the opera singer across the courtyard to pack it in,
"This is NYC, shithead, where fat people sing while fucking!"
Archie, whom Millie attacked with pliers
and Lizzie fell over, drunk on the stairs, angry
if you nodded or didn't, from whom, hearing his boots,
I hid shaking under the stairwell,
until I found him trembling outside my door,
"Scram, Zorro, I'll be peachy in the morning."
In a year three others here were dead of AIDS,
everyone wearing black
but in the West Village everyone did
every day anyway.

Patricia says, the Righteous Brothers and I
moved in Thanksgiving, 1977,
and immediately began looking for
that ever-loving feeling, rejoicing
at being a citizen of the ever-clanging future,
all of us walking up Perry Street,
down West 10th, around Bleecker,
along the Hudson, with dogs, girlfriends,
and hangovers, stoned and insanely sober,
arm in arm and solo, under the big skyline,
traffic whizzing by, through
indefatigable sunshine, snow and rain,
listening to the Stones, Monk, Springsteen, and Beethoven,

one buoyant foot after the other, nodding hello
good morning happy birthday adieu adios auf wiedersehen!
before anyone went co-op, renovated,
thought about being sick or dying,
when we all had hair and writhed on the floor
because someone didn't love us anymore,
when nobody got up before noon, wore a suit
or joined anything, before there was hygiene,
confetti, a salary, cholesterol,
or a list of names to invite to a funeral . . .

Yes, the adventures of a street in a city of everlasting hubris,
and Patricia's yellow light
when I can't sleep and come to the kitchen
to watch its puny precious speck stretch
so quietly so full of reverence
into the enormous darkness,
and I, overcome with love for everything so quickly fading,
my head stuck out the window
breathing the intoxicating melody
of our shouldered and cemented-in little island,
here, now, in the tenement of this moment,
dear Patricia's light,
night after night,
burning with all the others,
on 78 Charles Street.

Truth

You can hide it like a signature
or birthmark but it's always there
in the greasy light of your dreams,
the knots your body makes at night,
the sad innuendoes of your eyes,
whispering insidious asides in every
room you cannot remain inside. It's
there in the unquiet ideas that drag and
plead one lonely argument at a time,
and those who own a little are contrite
and fearful of those who own too much,
but owning none takes up your life.
It cannot be replaced with a house or car,
a husband or wife, but can be ignored,
denied, and betrayed, until the last day,
when you pass yourself on the street
and recognize the agreeable life you
were afraid to lead, and turn away.

The One Truth

After dreaming of radiant thrones
for sixty years, praying to a god
he never loved for strength, for mercy,
after cocking his thumbs
in the pockets of his immigrant schemes,
while he parked cars during the day
and drove a taxi all night,
after one baby was born dead
and he carved the living one's name
in windshield snow in the blizzard of 1945,
after scrubbing piss, blood,
and vomit off factory floors
from midnight to dawn,
then filling trays with peanuts,
candy, and cigarettes
in his vending machines all day,
his breath a wheezing suck
and bellowing gasp
in the fist of his chest,
after washing his face, armpits
and balls in cold backrooms,
hurrying between his hunger
for glory and his fear
of leaving nothing but debt,
after having a stroke and
falling down factory stairs,
his son screaming at him
to stop working and rest,
after being knocked down
by a blow he expected all his life,
his son begging forgiveness,
his wife crying his name,

after looking up at them
straight from hell, his soul
withering in his arms—
is this what failure is,
to end where he began,
no one but a deaf dumb God
to welcome him back,
his fists pounding at the gate—
is this the one truth,
to lie in a black pit
at the bottom of himself,
without enough breath
to say good-bye
or ask forgiveness?

Failure

To pay for my father's funeral
I borrowed money from people
he already owed money to.
One called him a nobody.
No, I said, he was a failure.
You can't remember
a nobody's name, that's why
they're called nobodies.
Failures are unforgettable.
The rabbi who read a stock eulogy
about a man who didn't belong to
or believe in anything
was both a failure and a nobody.
He failed to imagine the son
and wife of the dead man
being shamed by each word.
To understand that not
believing in or belonging to
anything demanded a kind
of faith and buoyancy.
An uncle, counting on his fingers
my father's business failures —
a parking lot that raised geese,
a motel that raffled honeymoons,
a bowling alley with roving mariachis —
failed to love and honor his brother,
who showed him how to whistle
under covers, steal apples
with his right or left hand. Indeed,
my father was comical.
His watches pinched, he tripped
on his pant cuffs and snored

loudly in movies, where
his weariness overcame him
finally. He didn't believe in:
savings insurance newspapers
vegetables good or evil human
frailty history or God.
Our family avoided us,
fearing boils. I left town
but failed to get away.

New Poems

Things I Have to Do Today

Check why my car's engine light keeps blinking,
shift two tutorials so I can attend Eli's play tomorrow,
make sure *Prometheus Bound* is by Aeschylus
so I won't confirm his growing suspicion of my ignorance.
Call Santos to patch and paint the upstairs ceiling leak,
get Monica to pick paint color before he gets too busy.
Congratulate Joel and Odette on publishing their first stories.
Adjust the basketball hoop before the boys grow any taller.
Finish reading the Norwegian novel about a man living alone
in the woods with his dog even though the voice is so at peace
with the trees and river and light it frightens me. Replace
the outside lights so raccoons don't get into our garbage,
clip Penelope's nails and find a way to help my students
be less afraid of what in them is most vulnerable, powerful,
and unwilling to settle. Find the courage to begin the poem
about a man at his window, trying to imagine a place
where the fragile chemistry of his happiness can survive
his envy, ignorance and guilt, where the poor aren't tricked
into believing poverty is a weakness and shame an inheritance,
where great wealth isn't made at the expense of the weak,
the naïve and the frightened, where his sons won't inherit
his anguish and ignominy, where his love for others is greater
than his pity for himself, where truth isn't despised by the bitter,
the angry and greedy, where everything he loves isn't lost forever,
where the fire can survive even the anger of the gods, unbound.

The Reasonable Houses of Osborne Lane

All the walking up and down, glancing about,
nodding hello good morning mild winter,
the sweet sisters set back nicely against their
ever-vanishing woods, dear Mr. Miller, Mrs. Lamb
and Mrs. Cobb, their stories about the ghosts of
potato farmers and the fickle pretty Irish pot-wallopers
in the rich kitchens, the pickups in the fancy shrubs
every Saturday night, their ecstasy heard on Main Street,
Jack next door tending his faithful garden, Joel tucked
inside their rose-haloed doorway, whistling to Figaro,
Barbara of the corner, planting Japanese ferns,
racked by the hysterical wisteria of divorce, cottages
slowly blooming into mansions, us strolling with Augie
lashed to your back, Eli holding my hand, our dogs sniffing
ants fungi bottle caps pounded into the history of cement,
through the anniversaries of our one remarkable idea,
the shade of elms maples lilac-flavored oaks, the Chevys
Buicks and Toyotas going north toward the woods and south
toward the ocean, the elegant sky springing to attention,
neighbors carried in and out of ambulances, the privacy of
long azure afternoons dragging shadows toward twilight,
kids selling a lemony innocence, the late and early singing
in the moon-drunk leaves, robins complaining to the squirrels
about their ceaseless roof dancing, the raked gravel scrape of
winter hoarding its ribald dreams toward one last invasion of color,
the shining over the always surprising blue light of morning.

Attention

More often than not, my wife deserves more
than I can give her, a balancing act of knowing
when to be visible, given her importance
to our complexity. My sons need less as they
grow older, one always less than the other.
My friends need more as they grow older.
The dead ones, especially. Even while asleep,
our dog needs some, tail beckoning. The more
our house gets, the more it needs. The walls
need to be thanked for their loyalty and patience,
the floors for suffering the weight of our indifference.
I try not to feel too bad about my students.
Guilt is essential to our relationship, guilt,
persistence and a great serenity. My poems
poach nearly everything, my fears, schemes,
conjectures and astonishments, after evidence
of infidelity, scraps of inspiration. Indifferent to
the suffering they describe, they dislike everything
I love, believe only in their insularity. Because
I never really had one before, my career never
used to ask for much. Now, disguised as letters,
emails, phone calls, it never lets me forget it's there,
a new best friend whose only purpose is to prove
its inevitability. There's our town, its politics, scandals
and obligations, and all the fine, inescapable privileges
of citizenship in an idea no one understands anymore.
And, yes, the wars, of course, their constant scraping
fork-tongued self-aggrandizing exaggerations. Also,
my happiness, its stubborn, perverse vulnerability
that tries not to call attention to itself. Sometimes,
late at night, we, my happiness and I, reminisce,
lifelong antagonists enjoying each other's company.

The Opening

Everyone arrives later than everyone else,
taller than expected, the gossip anthropological
in nature, turning clockwise. Stubborn,
the art doesn't seem to mind being the center
of its own attention. Death remains in fashion,
while delight appears to be making a comeback.
Art, the conversation claims, is "an assault on time,"
"a currency of doubt and opportunity," "a cease-fire
with calamity." Uninvited, it keeps on coming,
its mouth filled with intuition, such lovely feathers.
Ah, the white fluorescent walls, the landscapes grateful
to have survived their own stillness. Everyone seems
to want something, dogma, truth, a context, politics
is not out of the question, but passion twists the ephemeral
into perception, urges the phenomenal to confront
the merely mysterious. You know what I mean—all that
endless standing, stepping back, squinting, sighing, doing
and undoing, the middle torn out of its own beginning,
the pleading to be finished, finally, the fiery binge and hoist
of the impossible ingested, flattened to nothing, the honed figure
walking out the door, alone under the night's vast umbrella,
the hat complaining to the rectangle about its lack of grammar,
the hilarious despair of the square, the aluminum shiver longing
for the simplicity of the lowly nut and bolt, canvas stretched
across infinity, the disappointments, unbearable happiness,
beckoning for the feast to begin.

Aging Egoists

At dinner last night our hosts complained
about the expense of heating their pool,
keeping an army of unreliable gardeners
and handymen, the pain of being envied.
Everyone sought their largesse, they said.
My wife swims at the YMCA while I jog
along the ocean whose upkeep costs me
almost nothing. Experts in the art of possession,
they believe artists require, like children,
approval and forbearance. Apparently,
they expected gratitude, infantilism, and
a return on their investment; we expected
exceptional dry white wine, exquisite pâtés,
grandiosity, a little praise, and contempt.
The evening was a success. They hugged
and kissed us on both cheeks, we hugged
and kissed them back. Driving home,
we tried to imagine what might occur if truth
were apportioned like their view of the sea.
Were we all aging egoists, battling boredom
and death, despising what we longed for?
Oddly buoyed and estranged, we drove through
the long silence of the trees, utterly bewildered.

The Fourth of July

We'd pile into Dad's old blue Ford wagon and go
to Lake Ontario to watch the fireworks, Dad laughing
at something nasty Uncle Al said about Aunt Becky,
who just stood there, burning, Mom crying big laugh tears
at something Dad said about women like she wasn't one,
everyone eating as fast as they could, touching everyone else
maybe because the war was finally over and hard luck
was something you could despise and celebrate. No one knew
anything, Grandma said, spitting twice over her left shoulder.
We knew what we liked, watching our imaginary friends,
the clouds, Bull, Pigface and Spongy, swim over the horizon
on missions they never returned from, counting the enemies
they'd killed with their bare hands, the secrets they'd buried
with their medals. We'd sit in the sand, pretending it was okay
to squander the future, our happiness wouldn't lose sight of us.
Back then, everyone got mad if you said anything about America,
nobody thought his best wasn't good enough. Maybe that's why
we enjoyed exploding things, because we knew the war wasn't
really over, it was just resting, and most of our vows had already
been broken, and our one big idea was over two hundred years old
and everyone was tired of watching Uncle Al inflate his biceps
by blowing on his thumbs, hoping for just one more good idea.

Free Mercy

The woman beside me on the jitney weeps
into a cell phone, "You're leaving me!"
Every seat is taken, it's late, and I'm tired
so I rehearse objections as she cries, "Billy!
You love the way I swim! You love my eyes!"
I try a childhood distraction trick: my dog
Rusty runs away, it's my birthday and beautiful
Miss Crittenden, my fourth-grade teacher, is leaving
to get married . . . "Hear that?" the woman cries,
ripping a magazine. "It's my heart!" My father
dies bankrupt and I don't go to college . . . "That time
you saw the cuts on my wrist and asked if I'd do *that*
over you and I said no? I *was* lying." I stutter, lisp,
apologize too much . . . "I'm coming back to an empty house?"
My number is called, I'm going to Vietnam . . . "Billy, please,
a little mercy . . ."

Last Sunday my son got tired of skating so we walked
around the cemetery by the pond and stopped to read
a poem called "Free Mercy" inscribed on a stone in 1688,
about a boy who died at sea "innocent and happy," and
I wondered if it meant one shouldn't have to pay for it,
and we stood there, my wife, son, the baby, and me, each
a tiny piece of free luck, and all the kids skating behind us,
laughing, as if Miss Crittenden would never leave them.

Stein, in Produce

Over there, hiding behind the oranges,
giving some guy the same old line
about how we're all just a tiny piece
of a bigger picture, is my ex–guardian
angel Stein, blinking, spitting, shivering
the same old volatile symphony of tics.
Ah, this poor slob, Stein's latest salvation,
probably thinks he's hearing voices,
but soon enough he'll see a frayed,
sardines-stinking stout angel, mumbling
about how love isn't an invitation to sponges
and artfully aligned pyramids of detergents
eager to disinfect the future, but an obligation
to continue his own kind. Visible only to
the lost and self-neglected, Stein must be
weary of being an antidote to self-pity,
sexy as a bundle of budget diapers. Once
he performed best in girlie shows, where
the lonely practice the art of diversion.
Married with two boys, now I'm
a success story, my photo in his album
of *Happy Losers*. Sequestered behind beer
and pretzels, I watch him guide his recruit
through the glistening tomatoes and peaches
toward the luxuriously painful, ever-ripening
roses of love. I admit I'm jealous. Perhaps
the art of happiness is just another diversion?

The Joke

Today, a friend called to tell me a joke:
"Alec Baldwin lives near you, right?
Drive past his house and see if there's
a For Sale sign. He said he'd leave the country
if Bush got reelected." This is five days
after the election and he knows my wife and I
are suffering, that we fear raising children
in a world that hates them. Surprised,
I say nothing. He helped me make money once,
for which I'm grateful, and guilty.
He calls when the loneliness at the top of
the American mountain becomes intolerable,
and his great striving to be a tiny walled city
sours his sleep. I understand. He can't be
vulnerable with people he fears,
and therefore respects. Compassion
is a weakness, he thinks, my desire to give
is a kind of greed. That's why people like him
are in power, he'd argue, because people like me
have no stomach for war and death.
He's right. I don't hate my sensitivity,
as he hates his. High thought is impossible
without compassion, Socrates believed.
It asks us to love the minds of others as if
they were our own. War loves only itself.
Though he can't feel his pain, my friend
is suffering. That's why he told me this joke,
because gloating is his way of asking for sympathy,
something even all his money can't buy.
Ask and he'll say he loves me. Yes,
but like a village he must destroy in order to save.

Yom Kippur

You are asked to stand and bow your head,
consider the harm you've caused,
the respect you've withheld,
the anger misspent, the fear spread,
the earnestness displayed
in the service of prestige and sensibility,
all the callous, cruel, stubborn, joyless sins
in your alphabet of woe
so that you might be forgiven.
You are asked to believe in the spark
of your divinity, in the purity
of the words of your mouth
and the memories of your heart.
You are asked for this one day and one night
to starve your body so your soul can feast
on faith and adoration.
You are asked to forgive the past
and remember the dead, to gaze
across the desert in your heart
toward Jerusalem. To separate
the sacred from the profane
and be as numerous as the sands
and the stars of heaven.
To believe that no matter what
you have done to yourself and others
morning will come and the mountain
of night will fade. To believe,
for these few precious moments,
in the utter sweetness of your life.
You are asked to bow your head
and remain standing,
and say Amen.

The Sweet Undertaste

What accounts for the sweetness of human beings?
For the fragile, inexhaustible longing in the eyes
of the slowly dying, the sweet undertaste of
a tune sung in a moment of unutterable delight?
For the gentle, whimsical blue in Uncle Sigmund's eyes
after he kept falling on his one leg and was told
to stop drinking? For the strength to crawl bleeding
to the phone and open the door? For his bewildered,
bloodied hospital smile? Irony gets us only so far.
Bitterness exhausts the heart. Disappointment loves
only itself. What accounts for the ignorance and hate
that chased him from the German side of Poland
to the Russian side, from the honeycomb of innocence
to the boomeranging cold of a cattle car rushing through
the moonless Siberian night, from the wrong side of fate
to the unalterable fact that once a man has run for his life
never again can he sleep through the night, that once salvation
is torn out of us we continue to run, on one leg and two,
to crawl like a worm through the stony anonymous earth?
Yes, what in this tumultuous infinitely regenerative world
accounts for the sweetness of his pious smile though my wife,
two boys and I will soon leave and take our happiness with us,
and he'll remain here, in this childless hospital room, his liver
blackened with whisky, his left pant leg pinned at the knee,
surrounded by the ravenous dreams of the lost and misplaced,
and the ricocheting echoes of the world eight floors below?

The God of Loneliness

It's a cold Sunday February morning
and I'm one of eight men waiting
for the doors of Toys R Us to open
in a mall on the eastern tip of Long Island.
We've come for the Japanese electronic game
that's so hard to find. Last week, I waited
three hours for a store in Manhattan
to disappoint me. The first today, bundled
in six layers, I stood shivering in the dawn light
reading the new *Aeneid* translation, which I hid
when the others came, stamping boots
and rubbing gloveless hands, joking about
sacrificing sleep for ungrateful sons. "My boy broke
two front teeth playing hockey," a man wearing
shorts laughs. "This is his reward." My sons
will leap into my arms, remembering this morning
all their lives. "The game is for my oldest boy,
just back from Iraq," a man in overalls says
from the back of the line. "He plays these games
in his room all day. I'm not worried, he'll snap out of it,
he's earned his rest." These men fix leaks, lay
foundations for other men's dreams without complaint.
They've been waiting in the cold since Aeneas
founded Rome on rivers of blood. Virgil understood that
death begins and never ends; that it's the god of loneliness.
Through the window, a clerk shouts, "We've only five."
The others seem not to know what to do with their hands,
tuck them under their arms, or let them hang,
naked and useless. Is it because our hands remember
what they held, the promises they made? I know
exactly when my boys will be old enough for war.
Soon three of us will wait across the street at Target,
because it's what men do for their sons.

Bleecker Street

It's a lovely June afternoon
and I'm heading up Bleecker Street
for a hazelnut espresso latte,
the kind made out of real hazelnuts,
not syrup, hoping it will empty me
of all my bickering ideas about love
and fate and immortality
so I can hear the fertile songs of spring.
Miguel de Unamuno—whose name
is impossible to say without smiling—
believed "self-love widens into love of all that lives."
Thank God for Unamuno! For hazelnut lattes!
But the infinite archaeology of my stupidity
prefers the charms of self-pity
to the equilibrium of self-love.
Perhaps these three Chinese girls
giggling into cell phones, lavishly spending
each moment of their youth, truly believe
the mountain of self has no top
and each breath is a reckoning with fate?
Perhaps these shiny boutiques, each
so resolute, so eager to please, are weary
of decorating the illusions of another century,
prefer the runaway slaves they hid in their root cellars,
their dreams of slaughter and deliverance?
Perhaps this beautiful blond woman,
screeching to a stop in a lilac Mercedes,
pursued by wailing police cars, finally
understands that it is not only for the soul
but for the mind that happiness is a necessity?
"Is the rich bimbo stoned or just stupid?"
an old man, radiant with rage, screams.

Perhaps everyone secretly admires
something momentous about himself,
with the mass and "inner life" of a cathedral,
in the tradition of the Spanish saints and mystics
who cherished the bliss of infinite sacrifice?
Perhaps this street remembers the loneliness
of war widows, the roll calls of absent names,
its first kisses on the corner of West 10th Street,
the swooning confetti heat of victory,
the scalding springs of defeat? Indeed,
this street is a wave of advocacy
and streaming window peonies and tulips,
a fierce glimpse of history, an echoing
of nightly gunshots, a flag of black pigeons
flowing east toward the end of a continent,
a hunger for immortality, a tiny brusque city,
a bickering idea, a useless boutique,
a fertile song widening into a love for all that lives.

The Big Sleep

The only thing which consoles us for our miseries is diversion,
and yet this is the greatest of our miseries.

—PASCAL

On Turner Classic Movies Philip Marlowe
is grimacing at the slinky beauty
of the woman who will become
the wife of the actor playing him.
The man playing me, up at three this morning,
worrying about the cost of private school,
health insurance, and the slow grinding
away of his savings, is wearing
bleaching molds because a stain chart
listed his smile as second to worst.
On CNN quaint dioramas of Baghdad,
the Sudan and Gaza depict recent forms
of human misery. Is there a chart
that measures our ignorance and vanity?
On PBS philosophers are debating what
Nietzsche meant by our desire to create
beyond ourselves the purest will.
The sexual fire in the amber eyes
of the woman Lauren Bacall is playing,
perhaps? On the Western Channel
the whiteness of Joel McCrea's teeth
has survived dust storms, chewing tobacco,
and his character's nostalgia for
the brutality of his tiny moment. Some believe
we've consumed our originality,
that our diorama will depict nothing.
On the Disney Channel all fifty-six signers
of the Declaration of Independence
are shouting about the indignity of domination
for everyone except perhaps those

tending their fields and children.
Did the man playing Nietzsche grow weary
of trying to grow happiness out of pure will?
Hat over heart, the man playing my father
stood perpendicular to his exhausted,
uneducated, immigrant shadow, weeping
to our national anthem. A man stood for something,
he said. Did the actor playing Marlowe
understand that Marlowe stood for nothing?
On the History Channel men and beasts
are being slaughtered by machetes, explosions
and hangings, their swollen, mystified bodies
falling into ravines, dropping to their knees
screaming for their mothers and God to save them.
It's three in the morning and everywhere
around me the silence stands for nothing
and even the god playing God wants to sleep.

Acknowledgments

The new poems were previously published in the following magazines, to whose editors grateful acknowledgment is made: *Crazyhorse, Five Points, The New Yorker, Per Contra, Poetry Daily, Slate, The Southern Review, TriQuarterly.*

I wish to thank friends who offered helpful suggestions on many of these poems: Carl Dennis, Robert Pinsky, Sal Robinson and Drenka Willen of Houghton Mifflin Harcourt, and especially my wife, Monica Banks.

"Bleecker Street" is for Grace Schulman and Jerome L. Schulman
"Free Mercy" is for Tony Hoagland
"The Big Sleep" is for Mike Pride
"The Fourth of July" is for Gerald Stern
"The God of Loneliness" is for Wesley McNair
"The Opening" is for Connie Fox and William King
"The Reasonable Houses of Osborne Lane" is for Jack Ceglic and
    Manuel Fernandez-Casteleiro
"The Sweet Undertaste" is for Sigmund Heuberg
"Things I Have to Do Today" is for Bill and Genie Henderson

Index of Titles and First Lines